Brian Johnston

The authorised biography

Also by Tim Heald

Fiction

Unbecoming Habits
Blue Blood will out
Deadline
Let Sleeping Dogs Die
Just Desserts
Murder at Moose Jaw
Caroline R
Masterstroke
Class Distinctions
Red Herrings
Brought to Book
The Rigby File (*ed*)
Business Unusual
A Classic English Crime (*ed*)

Non-fiction

It's a Dog's Life
The Making of Space 1999
John Steed, the Authorised Biography Vol 1
HRH The Man Who Would be King
    (*with* Mayo Mohs)
Networks
The Character of Cricket
The Newest London Spy (*ed*)
By Appointment – 150 years of
    the Royal Warrant and its Holders
My Lord's (*ed*)
The Duke – A Portrait of Prince Philip
Honourable Estates
A Life of Love – The Life of Barbara Cartland

TIM HEALD

Brian Johnston

The authorised biography

Methuen

First published in Great Britain in 1995 by Methuen London
an imprint of Reed Books Ltd
Michelin House, 81 Fulham Road, London SW3 6RB
and Auckland, Melbourne, Singapore and Toronto

Grateful acknowledgement is made to the Estate of Brian Johnston for the
use of quoted material from his private papers and tape recordings
copyright © 1995 by the Estate of Brian Johnston

Grateful acknowledgement is also made to Pauline Johnston for providing
most of the photographs in this book. For some individual pictures, thanks
are due to:
The BBC for number 39; Patrick Eagar for numbers 40, 42 and 43; *Radio
Times* for number 32; and John Woodcock for numbers 33 to 37.

A CIP catalogue record for this book
is available at the British Library
ISBN 0 413 69320 1

Typeset by Deltatype Ltd, Ellesmere Port, Wirral
Printed and bound in England by
Clays Ltd, St Ives plc

Contents

Brian Johnston

Illustrations

Author's Note

I first met Brian Johnston at Headingley during a Test match against Australia just a few years before he died. I had been asked to write a magazine piece about *Test Match Special*, and Brian had agreed to be interviewed in the commentary box.

When we had finished our interview we went off to lunch, walking along the back of the Headingley ground which doubles up as the home of the Leeds rugby league football club. At one point Brian half tripped on a bench and said, quite angrily, 'Oh, bugger!' I remember the sense of relief. It was not a word he would ever have used on air or in public. For a moment that veneer of self-control had slipped. I thought to myself, 'Oh good, he's real.'

My next encounter was in 1989, when I was editing an anthology about Lord's Cricket Ground for MCC at the behest of E. W. Swanton. Although the fee was derisory Brian was happy to write about his favourite ground and contributed a typically charming, anecdotal piece. For forty-two years he had lived within walking distance of the ground – two minutes from the Cavendish Avenue house, eight and a half

Brian Johnston

from Hamilton Terrace and sixteen 'on a good day' from Boundary Road. That summer he commentated on his fifty-second Lord's Test which must, as he remarked, be why he thought of the place as 'My Lord's'.

Most of our communication was by post. His came in the form of blue postcards covered in spidery blue writing.

Thereafter I bumped into him from time to time at cricket grounds. We chatted at Wormsley on the opening day of John Paul Getty's magnificent country house ground, and we said an affable hello behind the pavilion at Lord's. He was always smiling, polite but faintly remote. In no way could I claim friendship. When he died I shared in the national mourning, but only as an acquaintance and admirer.

Then one day I came home and found a message scribbled in my younger son's handwriting. I was to ring someone called Pauline Johnston.

I duly telephoned and she explained that she was Brian's widow and was looking for someone to write a book about him. Would I be interested?

When I met Pauline and Brian's children it transpired that various other writers had been keen to write his life but there was a feeling within the family that there was more to Brian than cricket. Nearly all the other potential authors were very closely identified with the game and while it was obviously a passion of his he had other interests and loves. In later life Brian had become almost inextricably identified with *Test Match Special* and chocolate cake. I could see that they both loomed large but I sensed, as his family obviously felt, that any book about him should reflect his varied life as a whole.

Brian, of course, had written a good deal himself. In all, if you leave out a posthumous volume of jokes, he published fifteen books, all more or less autobiographical. Clearly these were an important source, especially *It's Been a Lot of Fun*, which he wrote immediately after his formal retirement from the BBC in the early 1970s. Brian disliked waste and when, some twenty years later, he wrote *Someone Who Was – Reflections on a Life of Happiness and Fun*, the material was rearranged into a different sequence – alphabetical rather than chronological – but otherwise remained substantially the same.

I had a slight problem with these books and in particular with Brian's polished anecdotes. Roy Hudd, in his foreword to Brian's final book of jokes described him, affectionately, as 'the wicked old poacher', and Brian made no bones about the fact that many of his jokes and routines had been picked up in the comedian's equivalent of the Oxfam shop. And from time to time they were lightly moulded to fit in with his own experience.

So there is, in these books, an element of fantasy and myth-making. Does this matter? Not if one is simply interested in entertainment. If, on the other hand, you want to know what Brian Johnston was *really* like, then the well honed patter can be frustrating.

I have tried to sort out the facts from the fantasy, particularly where it really does affect his life story. Two events in particular seem to me to be significantly under-played or distorted – the death of his father when he was a small boy and his winning of the Military Cross in the Second World War. It is all part of his constant attempt to be sunny and smiling no matter what. His own version of his life makes it look as if it was all wonderful, rollicking fun, with never a bleak moment or an untoward reverse. I think that was what he wanted us to believe and perhaps what he believed himself. But I'm not wholly convinced.

He kept diaries, but he was no Samuel Pepys or even Alan

Clark. His diaries were like most people's – small dog-eared books which fitted into a jacket pocket – and were used to log appointments. Lunches at Boodles, haircuts, Test matches, yes . . . but no revealing passages of introspection or reflection.

Nor was he a passionate letter-writer. He preferred postcards – often naughty seaside ones – which on the whole were no more easily decipherable than the diary entries. But most of his communication was oral. He was an assiduous telephonist in regular communication with a wide interconnected but carefully compartmentalised circle of friends.

And, of course, there are tape recordings of his famous one-man show and also of the various BBC broadcasts he made. These, though incomplete, go back to his very earliest days 'going somewhere' in the late 1940s. They are nearly always interesting but obviously aimed at the general public so that, on the whole, they reveal little of the inner man but are mainly a confirmation of the personality known to millions.

There are other published sources. Many of his fellow cricket commentators have written memoirs and autobiographies and all include a number of Johnston anecdotes – usually the same ones, though often told from a slightly different perspective. However the most valuable sources in this area have been various autobiographies by William Douglas-Home, possibly his greatest friend, but one who was often perceptive about Brian, albeit in the most affectionate way. Maddeningly, both William and Brian tell many of the same stories but frequently differ on several points. As they have both died and as there were often no other witnesses you simply have to pay your money and take your choice.

Another invaluable source is *Summers Will Never Be the Same*, the valedictory volume of tributes assembled by Christopher

Martin-Jenkins and Pat Gibson. Not surprisingly it is weighted in favour of the later years and of cricket.

The most tantalising sources have been those who knew him best. Here too there are dangers. Memory is often faulty, particularly at a distance of seventy odd years and without much chance of written corroboration. I confess I did become mildly dismayed sometimes when, arriving at the home of one of Brian's old school chums, one was greeted with infinite politeness, a glass of sherry and, 'I'm afraid I'm not going to be able to tell you anything you don't know already', or, 'You'll know all the stories by now', or, 'The thing about Brian is that what you saw was what you got. No hidden depths there . . . Ha! Ha! Ha!'

His immediate family were the most revealing. Pauline and the children were generous with their time and disarmingly honest in their recollections. They obviously loved him very much, but this did not blind them to his eccentricities and foibles.

Partly because, despite some modern newspaper obituarists, it is still bad form to speak ill of the newly dead, many of those to whom I spoke tended to be quite bland. It is not part of my brief to suggest that Brian wasn't an extremely nice man, but even among those who might be expected not to enjoy those jokes or sympathise with his conservative and Conservative tendencies there was a palpable reluctance to saying anything remotely critical. It was as if one were inviting someone to make a rude remark about the Queen Mother.

I hope this doesn't sound churlish. Almost everyone I asked for help was charming and hospitable and demonstrably fond of Brian. At the same time they nearly all seemed perfectly happy to accept the version according to Brian, the one he spent all his life perfecting. This, I concede, was part of the story, but I am still not convinced that it was the whole story. His was an almost constantly urbane, even suave façade, but I hope I managed to get a glimpse of the man behind the manner. I think there *was* more to him than met the eye. That doesn't make him any the less admirable or likeable but it may make him more complicated, interesting, brave and, perhaps above all, mysterious.

Prologue

May 16th 1994. It was a typically early cricket season sort of day: no rain to interfere with play, but enough crispness in the air for sweaters. It was the sort of weather Brian would have associated with the first match of the summer tour at Worcester.

Half an hour before play was due to begin, the queue stretched hundreds of yards back from the Great West Door of Westminster Abbey. It snaked all along the railings into Parliament Square and it contained the great and the good and the plain ordinary, which was just how he would have wished it. The Secretary of MCC, Roger Knight, and the President of MCC, Dennis Silk, alighted from their taxi at 11.30 at almost exactly the same time as a tousled David Gower, grinning in that characteristically sheepish way as he walked to the back of the queue.

'How did you know him?' I asked my neighbour as we shuffled towards our pews.

'Oh, I didn't,' he said, 'but I admired him.'

Brian would have enjoyed the ties, for he had a penchant

for old-fashioned meaningful stripes. There were rhubarb and custard MCC ties, and duck egg and black Old Etonian ties, and Lord's Taverners ties and Eton Ramblers ties and hundreds of others signifying membership of cricket clubs obscure and famous. 'I thought of wearing my MCC tie,' confided the Prime Minister a little later, 'but I thought it might look like showing off.'

The Abbey Church was packed out. Indeed it was a mightier congregation than you would find at most county championship matches these days, especially on a Monday morning in May.

The service itself was billed as a 'celebration', so that although it had its solemn moments there was laughter and fun as well, which was surely as he would have wished. The band of his old regiment, the Grenadier Guards, played the 'Eton Boating Song', and provided the most affecting moment of the service when two soldiers, one on fife and one on drum, slow marched the length of the church playing that soulful regimental lament, 'The Grenadier's Return'. Each of his three sons, Barry, Andrew and Ian, gave readings – verses by his old friend William Douglas-Home, a passage on the meaning of life from his own book, *Someone Who Was*, and a foreword to another of his books by Bud Flanagan. Colin Cowdrey and John Major both spoke. Trollope was invoked. And the Grantland Rice poem which ends with the sentiment that it matters not who won or lost – 'but how you played the game'. Lord Runcie, the former Archbishop of Canterbury, led us in thanking God for him; Richard Stilgoe recited some verses he had composed specially for the occasion; Michael Denison read Neville Cardus on the Long Room at Lord's; and Melvin Collins read his own poem – 'Johnners – From a Blind Listener'. The service ended on a characteristically

2

Johnstonian note. It must have been the first time that the theme from *Neighbours* and 'Underneath the Arches' were played in the Abbey church. Brian's musical tastes were always catholic. The Dean had agreed to these selections, on condition that he didn't actually have to process down the aisle to the tune of an Australian soap opera.

Afterwards a host of his friends adjourned to the Banqueting House in Whitehall for a jolly lunch. Pauline had asked that ladies should wear 'bright clothes', and she herself set a good example by wearing vivid pink and also making a festive speech of thanks of which Brian would have been proud.

The room was full of laughter and at the end of the buffet meal strawberry and banana messes, the traditional Eton summer pudding, were handed round.

'Can I get you a drink?' someone asked Brian's old friend, Denis Compton, the greatest living English cricketer, who was limping heavily on a single crutch.

'No thanks old boy,' said Compton. 'The Prime Minister's getting me one.'

And, sure enough, Mr Major presently appeared with a glass of red wine from the bar.

It was an exchange which Brian Johnston would have enjoyed. It was all too easy to imagine him chortling at the idea of the Prime Minister being Compton's personal wine waiter. He relished that sort of mild and wholly English absurdity, just as he relished life in all its richness and variety, always taking rough with smooth, though kidding the rest of us that there was no such thing as rough.

Once or twice in that convivial throng someone said something which brought back a memory of 'Johnners' so vividly that for a second or so there were tears amid the

3

laughter. That seemed right too. They were wiped away quite fast, but it was meant to be a poignant occasion as well as fun.

The great sadness was that he was not there to share in the jokes and the reminiscences and the fondness of friendship recalled. And yet, of course, he *was* there, lingering on in everyone's mind, that utterly distinctive voice and character, symbolising so much of what was good about England, especially on a summer's day. Few others ever have so effectively talked their way into the nation's affection, and for those thousands who, through his broadcasting, came to think of him as their personal friend he'll never really be that far away. As another Etonian writer put it,

> Still are thy pleasant voices, thy nightingales, awake,
> For death he taketh all away, but them he cannot take.

Brian himself might have thought that a little far-fetched and over the top. In any case, he would probably protest, you couldn't possibly say his voice was like a nightingale's – more like an amusing auk or a humorous macaw.

But I think, deep down and perhaps without even acknowledging it, he would have known what I mean.

1

Silver Spoon

The Little Boy in the Big House

In later life one of Brian's great gifts was to fulfil most of the requirements of Kipling's 'If'. In particular he had the ability 'to talk with crowds and keep your virtue . . . walk with Kings – nor lose the common touch'.

He always seemed completely at ease with everyone from the dustman to the Duke and yet he was, undeniably, born with a silver spoon rammed firmly in his mouth. His friend and sparring partner, Don Mosey, who came from uncompromisingly humble Yorkshire origins, used to say to him, 'You've never had to struggle.' Like most of those who encountered Brian, Mosey didn't hold it against him, as he did with other silver spoonees, but there is no getting away from the fact that Brian was born privileged.

In the rarefied pecking order of the English class system the Johnston family probably stood somewhere on the border between 'upper-middle' and 'upper'. Their antecedents were ancient and their circumstances comfortable.

Earlier Johnstons were grander than Brian's immediate family, for in the seventeenth century the main branch was elevated to the peerage and became the Lords Johnston of Lochwood. As the name suggests, this was a Scottish title. Brian's distant ancestry was not, as his voice and manner might suggest, Home Counties English, but Lowland Scots. Subsequently they did better still, becoming first Earls and then Marquises of Annandale. Another cadet branch of the family, the Johnstones of Westerhall, became baronets and fabulously rich, but the seventh baronet managed to 'dissipate' it in 1912. The Westerhall family tended to spell their name with an 'e' unlike the senior branch and Brian himself.

Annandale, a few miles north of Lockerbie, in the Scottish border county of Dumfries, was where the first Johnstons, believed to be of Norman descent, received a grant of lands in the twelfth century. That land was called Johnston, and they built a great house there called Lochwood, now ruined.

Apart from Johnstons, Brian could claim one or two intriguing ancestors who married into the family. These included, in the seventeenth century, the granddaughter of a 'celebrated Borderer' called Auld Wat of Harden and his wife Mary, who was known as 'The Flower of Yarrow', as well as a number of cattle rustlers. Strangely, Brian never alluded to these colourful sounding characters when talking about his family tree – which, actually, doesn't seem to have been something which enormously interested him.

His mother's maiden name was Alt. The Alts seem to have been resolutely upper middle class and included explorers, Oxford dons and an Air Chief Marshal. His uncle, Brian Alt, was killed in the Boer War, and Brian was named after him.

On the Johnston side, the first of Brian's ancestors to move south seems to have been a Francis Johnston who was born in 1757 and died in 1828. He was the father of nine children, including Edward Johnston, who founded the Johnston family coffee company which was to play a significant part in Brian's life and of which more later.

Apart from the coffee merchants, Brian's Victorian family tree is dominated by Army officers, the occasional clergyman, and even a Fellow of All Souls College, Oxford – Henry Wakeman, son of Sir Offley Penbury Wakeman, Bart. Brian's grandfather, Reginald, who was in his mid-sixties when Brian was born, had been Governor of the Bank of England a couple of years earlier.

Into this interesting old family, now very much a Home Counties clan, Brian was born on 24 June 1912 at the Old Rectory, Little Berkhamstead. His father, Charles, was thirty-four at the time. His mother, Pleasance, came from a similar sort of background, her father being Colonel John Alt, CB. Brian was the fourth and last of their children. The eldest was his sister Kathleen Anne – invariably known by her second name – and two brothers, Michael and Christopher, born, respectively, in 1908 and 1910.

The family moved before the outbreak of the First World War, so Brian never really had any memories of the Old Rectory. The new house, also in Hertfordshire, was a sizeable mansion called Little Offley House. Brian describes it as 'a lovely Queen Anne house', but actually it seems to have been a typical English mixture of styles and periods including tall Jacobean chimneys and a fine William and Mary front door. His brother, Christopher, has described it as having Tudor origins with a Queen Anne front. In any event he too recalls it as being 'lovely'.

With Little Offley House went 500 acres of farmland and although the village was half-way between Hitchin and Luton, this was in Brian's time very much part of rural England. Many of his earliest memories were of 'calving, bulls

7

having rings put through their noses, and large farm horses being shod'. The family wagon was pulled by two prizewinning shires named Boxer and Beauty. Brian once rescued a black piglet, the runt of the litter, which the pigman was going to kill, and took it to his mother's bedroom. On another occasion he fell off a cart during haymaking and developed periostitis, a bruising of the membrane of the bone.

Pleasures were simple and old-fashioned. Brian used to remember rat-catching with dogs and sticks, and being allowed to 'help' with harvesting. Almost best of all was being allowed to stand on the 'up' platform at Hitchin when the Flying Scotsman came pounding through 'with steam belching out and the wheels of the train going biddle-de-dum, biddle-de-dum, biddle-de-dum'. On Sundays he and the others would walk one and a half miles to church, leave the dog at the Post Office, collect the vicar, Mr Gatty, and try not to giggle during his sermon. If they succeeded it was meringues for tea.

Brian, as nearly always, made those early years sound quite idyllic. Even the war was dismissed simply as 'uneventful except for one bomb which was dropped on Hitchin and killed a chicken'. Somehow this is typically Brian. Yet his father was serving on the Western Front for the duration and was seldom at home. He was a Lieutenant-Colonel and won the Distinguished Service Order as well as the Military Cross, which his son, Brian, was also to be awarded in the Second World War. His father's absence on dangerous active service must have been a concern and a worry. In 1915 his uncle Geoffrey was killed in France while serving with the Essex Yeomanry, aged only twenty-six. Brian, then three, would have been too young to have a very clear idea of what was going on.

Although there was plenty of farm produce, his mother insisted that they stick to rationing along with everyone else. So there were meat coupons, maize bread, maize pudding, and they even ate dandelions instead of lettuce.

After the war, life reverted to normality, though because of a crisis in the coffee business Colonel Johnston was compelled to work unsociably long hours in the City. He used to commute by train although he owned one of the original Ford 'Tin Lizzies' which would transport him to and from the station, as well as a Fiat Landaulet built by the local garage, which was capable of astonishing speeds of over fifty miles per hour.

The chauffeur's name was Wakefield. In addition there was a groom to look after his father's hunter, a gardener and boy, a butler, a parlourmaid, a housemaid, a 'tweeny' and a cook. Sixty years later Brian looked back on all this with amazement. For all his fame and success he himself was never able to maintain an establishment on anything like this lavish scale.

This charmed family life could not go on for ever. First Michael and then Christopher went off to boarding school. For a while Brian shared a succession of governesses with his sister. Brian always blamed Anne for the high turnover in governesses. The average was apparently two or three a year. Brian claimed that he was less trouble than she was, but he used to dread 'those wet kisses' when he went to say good-night. This dread of 'wet kisses' remained with him and became one of his standing jokes within his own family.

Eventually he, like his brothers, was judged too old for a governess at home. A new stage in his life was set to begin.

2

Golden Tongue

Grove of Academe

Sir James Barrie once said that 'nothing that happens after we are twelve matters very much'. The remark is quoted, with evident approval, on the flyleaf of the official history of Brian's preparatory school, Temple Grove.

In Brian's case it is obviously an exaggeration and yet it has an element of truth. What happened to him before he was twelve mattered very much indeed, and in many ways he remained throughout the remaining seventy odd years of his life very much the same person as the little boy at Temple Grove.

It was an old and rather grand establishment, founded in 1810, and originally housed in Lord Palmerston's old house in East Sheen between Mortlake and Richmond Park. It is now in a house just south of the Ashdown Forest, but in Brian's day it was in Eastbourne, near the Saffrons cricket ground, where it moved in 1907.

Something of its character may be guessed from the fact that the school played an annual cricket match against the Etonian old Temple Grove boys. A famous old boy was

Cornet Bankes of the 7th Hussars, who was awarded one of the first posthumous VCs at Lucknow in 1858. Others included Lord Grey of Fallodon and M.R. James. A former music teacher had been Sir Arthur Sullivan, composer of the Savoy Operas. Another famous Temple Grove product was Douglas Bader, a few years senior to Brian. Brian remembered him as a brilliant cricketer whose exploits were rewarded with a series of celebratory half holidays.

Brian arrived to join his elder brothers in 1920 when he was eight years old.

The official story is that most old boys looking back on their schooldays much preferred Temple Grove to the public school which followed. This doesn't seem to be the case with Brian who always said he adored Eton but remembered Temple Grove as 'pretty tough', with the 'usual amount of bullying'. There was a peculiarly unpleasant initiation ceremony which took the form of a concert in which all the new boys had to recite or sing. If they faltered the senior boy present hit them on the head with a large book.

Even at this stage in his life Brian was displaying a precocious ability to make people laugh. His brother Christopher remembers this from the earliest years. As Brian used freely to admit, he could tell bad jokes which amused everyone and led, usually, to him getting off more lightly than his fellows. The standard of joke can be gauged from the one about the headmaster's eye. The Rev. H. W. Waterfield, otherwise known as 'The Bug', had lost an eye while playing squash. The school joke, which assumed the status almost of a mantra, ran as follows:

'The Bug has got a glass eye.'
'Really – how do you know?'

12

'It came out in the conversation.'

This strikes me as a prototype Johnston joke.

The school at this time seems to have run on Latin, Greek, team games and corporal punishment. The Bug beat Brian once, giving him two of the best with 'a thick short cane which looked like a rhinoceros whip'. Mr Fritch regularly beat boys over the head with his knuckles – a painful practice known as a 'fiddler fotch'. Mr Bellamy had a round ebony ruler and also used to hit boys across the head. Mr Taylor kept a cane under his desk, contrary to school rules, but one day a daring boy called Corrie took it away from him and broke it across his knee.

Many phrases and customs were derived from Latin or Greek. At the end of every term, for instance, there was an informal auction of unwanted possessions with the vendor calling out 'Quis?' and the bidders shouting, 'Ego!' The school song, 'Omne Bene', was in Latin, though only the first verse seems to be seriously translatable. It runs:

'Omne bene, sine peona
Tempus est ludendi;
Venit hora absque mora
Libros deponendi.'

This, more or less, means: 'All is well, it is time for playing without punishment; the hour is coming without delay for putting away books.'

By the penultimate verse we are in deep linguistic waters:

Horum scorum sancti morum,
Harum scarum ibo,

13

Brian Johnston

> Rag tag, willy willy wag,
> Hic haec hoc redibo.

Then all attempt at Latin was abandoned, and the song ended:

> Jolly good song and jolly well sung,
> And jolly companions everyone:
> Holla, boys, holla, boys this is the day,
> Holla, boys, holla, boys, hip hip hooRAY.

This, like the school joke, strikes me as very Brian. The word 'jolly', for instance, remained an important part of his vocabulary throughout the rest of his life. And he always enjoyed jingly lines and rhymes. Temple Grove, naturally, had its own variation of one of the common chants of the English prep school, certainly from 1920, when Brian first joined, up to 1957, when I left a similar establishment.

> This time next week where shall I be?
> Not in this academee:
> No more Latin, no more Greek,
> No more cane to make me squeak,
> No more German, no more French,
> No more standing on the bench,
> No more greasy bread and butter,
> No more water from the gutter,
> No more spiders in my tea
> Making googly eyes at me!

Food at boarding school has always been a cause of complaint. Brian used to put down the awfulness and paucity of the Temple Grove food to the fact that the war had only just ended. It seems more likely that the fault was endemic. Brian's parents, like those of other boys, supplemented his rations with a termly 'Tuck Box' and regular supplies of biscuits and 'Marmite'. Marmite on those days came in a white jar, unlike the treacle brown one of today, and was pronounced 'Marmeat'. Brian continued to have Marmite with practically everything for the next seventy years.

Like many pupils at boarding schools, the Temple Grove boys made a regular running joke out of the school cuisine, something Brian was to do at the expense of his wife's cooking years later. The taps on the cocoa urn at Temple Grove were popularly supposed to be placed so high that the dregs could be used for making the following Sunday's chocolate pudding; tapioca was fish eyes or frogspawn; mince pies contained old gloves; mincemeat was alleged to be hashed cat or rat; dogs' graves in the grounds were supposed not to be canine at all but to contain the remains of former Temple Grove pupils who had died from malnutrition. And so on.

The Rev. Waterfield had taken the school over in 1902, supervised the move to Eastbourne and introduced a number of reforms. Hitherto there had been an impossibly arcane system of coloured caps and cap-bands, all designating tiny steps in the hierarchical ladder. At the instigation of Mrs Waterfield ('Mrs Bug') the multicoloured caps were abolished at a stroke and replaced by a single black and green one. According to Brian she had an enormous bottom, walked almost parallel to the ground on account, possibly, of arthritis, and was scarcely seen except on the last bath night of term, when she made sure everyone was returned home clean behind the ears.

Matron had a bosom as enormous as Mrs Bug's bottom,

allowed Brian to listen to her cat's whisker radio, on which he first heard a comedian called 'Stainless Stephen,' and once stole or 'confiscated' a packet of his illegal BDV cigarettes. These were very mild, and Brian and his chums used to smoke them behind the fives courts. He didn't care for them much so their loss was no great problem. Matron's dentures were notoriously insecure.

There was also, believe it or not, a school butler called Wilkins who had entered service with the Waterfields as a page boy in 1877. He always, of course, wore morning dress and had a single strand of wispy grey hair arranged across a pink pate.

Electricity and central heating were not introduced until two or three years after Brian left. All lighting was by 'incandescent' gas mantles.

There was a school Cadet corps run by Chief Petty Officer Crease, whose party trick was a back somersault into the school swimming bath executed while smoking his pipe. He taught Brian to swim, balanced on a canvas halter at the end of a rope, and rewarded him with a penny bar of 'Devona' toffee-flavoured chocolate when he managed his first unassisted breadth of the bath. Swimming, however, was never one of Brian's strengths. He never really progressed beyond a rudimentary dog-paddle. CPO Crease also taught him to shoot and he performed regularly with the school second VIII. Colonel Mitford, the CO, also reported that 'Platoon Drill under Sergeant Johnston and Sergeant Hearn was very good.'

Cricket was already his great love, and according to the school magazine he kept wicket 'very successfully' for the first XI in his two final years. His batting was more suspect: 'An eccentric bat and a bad judge of a run.' This remained the verdict on his cricket throughout his life. His lifelong friend, Sir Edward Ford, one-time tutor to King Farouk, and Assistant Private Secretary to Queen Elizabeth, told me in his study a mile or so from Brian's final home that his idea of batting was to charge down the wicket, hope to get a touch and, if so, to career on down the wicket, irrespective of the consequences for his partner. It was huge fun but not quite cricket in the accepted sense.

In his final year, however, his batting improved and he had a top score of 32. He was judged to have been a 'very efficient' keeper who could 'take the ball well on both sides and has caught and stumped a good many victims'. He was also praised for his 'never failing keenness' – which sounds right. At rugby he was described as a stand-off 'with plenty of brains'. He possessed a gratifying turn of speed even then, and later, when he ran at Oxford, he used to claim that he had a sprinter's ankles.

The Temple Grove Newsletter reported in its obituary of Brian that 'Very little is recorded about Brian's academic progress other than a comment in one report that "he talks too much in school".' Indeed to some of his schoolboy contemporaries he was known simply as 'The Voice'.

Plus ça change!

All this is fairly conventional and predictable stuff. He was clearly a 'card' with easy charm and the gift of the gab; keen on games; perfectly able to pass muster in the class-room without, one feels, exerting himself unduly; and operating in the context of a school which was only just emerging from the Victorian era but was nevertheless par for the upper-middle-class course of the age.

When he was ten, however, he experienced a tragedy

which was far from being conventional, predictable or typical in any way.

3

While Bathing at Bude

A Family Tragedy

Every summer the Johnstons took a family holiday in North Cornwall. They sound idyllically happy in a very typically English upper-middle-class fashion. There is a whiff of Arthur Ransome and *Swallows and Amazons* about those holidays, with perhaps a dash of Dornford Yates and a little Betjeman. The family was almost large enough to constitute a party in itself, but in addition there always seemed to be house guests.

Brian's brother, Christopher, told me that it was his mother who arranged the summer house in Bude. It was always the same house. 'I suppose we must like continuity,' said Christopher. 'My grandmother had always gone to Bude for summer holidays. Then my mother did. So did I, and now my daughter goes there.'

The pleasures were simple. There was golf, there was tennis but most of the fun centred on the beach; shrimping nets, cricket, buckets and spades, jam sandwiches with nutty grains of sand inevitably gritted in with the strawberries, saffron buns and cake. Brian had a memory of himself and his brothers constructing a sort of spaghetti junction of tunnels and bridges on the Bude beach into which they inserted a collection of white mice. This complex piece of engineering attracted a large crowd 'who watched them scampering in and out of the tunnels and over the bridges'.

Christopher says they brought the mice down on the train in tins. The arena on the beach was about the size of half a tennis court. 'People used to come from miles to watch. They could never understand why it was free.' Later they did the same thing with ferrets.

Naturally they played cricket, though their father seldom joined in. He was a rowing man who had twice won a blue, in 1898 and 1899, while up at New College, Oxford. Christopher told me that it was his brothers, Michael and 'Bri' who were the cricket fanatics. Christopher did not enjoy the game, much preferring anything to do with horses. However, he was invariably roped in, though most of the time he was happy doing his own thing with his 'useful' dog.

In 1922, when Brian was just ten years old, the happy holiday jollity was suddenly ruined. As the local newspaper later reported in the bathetic tones which local newspapers so often adopt for tragedy they cannot wholly comprehend, 'Quite a gloom was cast over Bude on Sunday evening.'

The day had begun well. Brian's father, the Colonel, had in fact been intending to return to London in order to resume work, but the weather improved so dramatically that morning that he decided to stay on and make the most of it. As usual there were a number of house guests among the party, including several old service friends of Colonel Johnston's.

They were on the beach at Widemouth sands and at low tide they all went swimming. There was a heavy sea, and at low tide off the North Cornish coast the undertow is strong and the currents are treacherous. Brian's sister, Anne, swam out too far and got into difficulties. Seeing this the Colonel and a family cousin, Lieutenant Walter Eyres, swam out to rescue her. It was arduous work and they were swimming against the tide.

Eyres seems to have been a stronger swimmer than the Colonel and it was mainly thanks to him that Anne was finally pulled ashore. During the struggle, however, the Colonel began to slip behind and it was obvious that he was in serious trouble. Another of the party, Captain Scully, had already left the water and was dressed. Hearing cries for help, Scully undressed again and went back into the sea to help with the rescue.

A rope was found from somewhere and Scully swam out towards the Colonel holding on to one end while the rest of the group stood on the shore holding on to the other end with the intention of pulling the Colonel to safety. What follows sounds pitifully chaotic. The rope was too short and communications between Scully and the men on the shore were hopeless. They pulled at the wrong moment, causing Scully to slip under the waves. Try as he might he could not reach the drowning man, and eventually the wretched Colonel drifted out to sea and out of sight.

At the inquest a few days later the Coroner recorded the obvious and inevitable verdict of death by drowning and said, a trifle bleakly, that he would try to get a notice put up warning of the dangers of swimming at low tide.

An odd twist to this sad story was that a year or so later Mrs Johnston remarried. Her second husband was none other than the man who had failed to rescue the Colonel, Captain Marcus Scully.

In later life Brian seems never to have talked about the incident. About his stepfather he was usually laconically

21

dismissive. 'Ah, Scully!' said Lord Carrington. 'Brian always used to say, "Scully finally left through the scullery window." ' This seems to have been true, at least metaphorically. The marriage was unsatisfactory and short-lived. When Scully finally left Brian's mother she stopped using his name and reverted to being Mrs Johnston.

Brian seldom talked about any of this. I did find one old schoolfriend who claimed to remember him making a black joke out of it. He remembered Brian saying something to the effect that he wouldn't have been surprised to learn that Scully had not only failed to rescue Colonel Johnston but that he actually drowned him. Held him under water . . . 'Glug, glug, glug'.

Apart from this no one that I spoke to could remember Brian ever having mentioned his father at all. Christopher told me that the death had a devastating effect on him and that he was sure it did on Brian as well. They were sharing a bedroom that summer and he still remembers the terrible grief that night with vivid clarity. Afterwards, however, none of the children ever referred to the tragedy. It was simply too painful.

It is also true that Brian can never have known his father tremendously well. The Great War began when Brian was just two years old, so between the ages of two and six he would have been effectively fatherless. Between 1920 and 1922 the Brazilian economy was in such disastrous shape that the very future of the family company was at risk and the Colonel had to labour night and day to ensure that it remained solvent. He can have had only limited time for family life.

Brian acknowledged as much in his first autobiography in 1974. 'I never got to know him as well as the modern boy knows his father,' he remarked. Christopher told me that their father was a distant, slightly gloomy seeming figure. He thinks that he was probably very affected by his experiences during the war. As he says, for a territorial officer to win a DSO and an MC is quite unusual. However, such gallantry has its price, and he thinks his father was damaged by what he saw and experienced himself in the trenches of the battlefields in northern Europe.

In his own book Brian describes his father's death in a manner which differs from the contemporary newspaper account in at least one important respect. In the newspaper version it is Brian's sister Anne who gets into trouble. Scully had emerged from the water and was changed. He had to undress again and then go back into the water to try to rescue the Colonel.

In Brian's own version, however, there is no mention of his sister getting into difficulties. Nor of Scully leading the rescue. Instead it is Scully, 'badly wounded in the war', who got caught in the drag and swept out to sea. In Brian's version it is his strong-swimming father who heroically dived in to rescue Scully. This is a very different story and reflects incomparably less well on Scully, who was not a great success either as a husband or a stepfather.

In his book Brian describes his father as 'quiet, honest, strict but kind and highly respected by all who knew him'. But he only devoted a few lines to him, and it is clear that he never really had the chance to get to know him. After his death one of his business colleagues wrote of him that he 'applied an austere diligence with a very high sense of duty'. This makes him sound admirable but not exactly comfortable. Years later in his one-man show Brian used to pay tribute to the important role his family played in his life. He spoke with affection of his mother and father, making no reference to the fact that he lost the latter as a little boy. Those shows were meant to be happy, enjoyable events and it would have been inappropriate to cloud them with tragic tales. All the same the image of a tranquil, safe, idyllic childhood Brian's words evoke seems to present less than the whole truth.

I was intrigued by the trauma Brian appears to have suffered to such an extent that I consulted one of Britain's leading child pyscho-therapists to see what her theories might be. In a sense I was lucky because she turned out to be American and therefore knew nothing whatever about Brian.

At first, as she readily admitted, she was not especially interested in my story, but the more I told her the more fascinated she became. I am as sceptical as most Englishmen of a certain age, upbringing and education, about psychology, psychiatry, counselling, therapy and the rest. I am sure Brian had that scepticism to an even more marked degree than myself and I concede that in this case we were, inevitably, talking hypothetically about a person who could not provide his own invaluable insight and information.

For these and other reasons I am reluctant to give my expert's opinions *too* much weight. She herself would also, I think, be tentative. When, for example, she offered a suggestion such as 'He almost seems to have *become* his father and to have taken the whole world on as his family,' there was a strong hesitation in her voice. It was, she appeared to be saying, an interesting notion, but in the circumstances it could hardly be more than an idea.

However, she was in no doubt that his father's death would have been a deeply shocking event for a ten-year-old boy and one which could not fail to inform his life. The fact that Brian never talked about it serves to confirm rather than deny the idea. The bereavement would have been shocking and formative in any case, but the fact that the family were forced to sell their house and never again really had a permanent home would have made it worse. That his father's place was usurped by the very man who failed to rescue him would have compounded the effect still further.

At the inquest one witness told the coroner that he was only giving evidence because so many rumours had been flying around. He wished to set the record straight. The nature of these rumours was not specified, but in view of the subsequent marriage between Scully and Mrs Johnston it seems likely that unpleasant gossip would have involved an earlier liaison between the two. I asked Christopher about this, but he shook his head and said he was far too young to have known about such things. Subsequently I asked his wife, Barbara, and she told me that her information was that the relationship between Scully and Mrs Johnston was the talk of the county.

Scuttlebutt or truth? We shall probably never know.

Christopher Johnston told me that he thought the family had 'a sneaking regard' for Scully. He seems to have had charm. He loved country pursuits and instructed his step-children in shooting and hunting and fishing. I asked if he had ever had a job, and Christopher thought for a moment and said 'No'. Perhaps his war wounds prevented honest toil. But, no, Scully had never had what you might call a job. He taught them to play bridge, a game which Brian played in adulthood with his own family. 'Dad always said that he really taught himself and learned as he went along,' says his daughter Clare.

Christopher told me Scully taught them.

No one seems to know what finally happened to Scully after the scullery window departure. Christopher recalls that his step-father once invited him to lunch at his club during the Second World War. That was his last sighting.

My psychotherapist's view is that much of Brian's approach to life would have been his way of dealing with all this. He himself would not have been aware that he was doing so. There would have been no conscious repression of past history, no wakeful early morning hours of lamentation. But, without realising it, his whole attitude to life and its problems would have been dictated by the awful events off the beach at Bude in 1922.

In a sense this has to remain relatively unknown and speculative territory, but as I considered his apparently ever effervescent life I was always mindful of that scar buried deep in his past. I was conscious of a deep-rooted hurt which never seems to have showed but which must have been there nonetheless.

4

Floreat Etona

A Wonderful Club

Brian adored Eton. He was not the only Etonian to look back on his days at school as some of the happiest of his life although this is not universal. Lord Howard de Walden arrived at exactly the same time as a new boy in the same house and remembers some aspects of Eton life as being distinctly disagreeable. The house was in the charge of a man called R. H. de Montmorency. Years later Montmorency's daughter, Ann, married Brian's cricket commentating colleague E. W. Swanton.

'Montmorency was about 102,' de Walden told me, exaggerating, but only slightly. 'They let some people stay on for ever in those days. He didn't pay any attention to what was going on so the house was run by the boys at the top who were a pretty nasty lot.' He remembers cold baths every morning and also recalled, vividly, that he was once beaten 'for looking as if I owned the place'. He says he never forgave the boy who did it.

There is nothing new in this contrasting view of public school in general and Eton in particular. A few years before

Brian's arrival an Old Etonian father, talking to his two teenage sons on the eve of the younger one's first 'half' at the school, mused: 'For my part I am sure the happiest days of my life were spent there; and there is no reason to expect that Charley will find it otherwise if only he keeps out of scrapes, avoids debts and is sufficiently industrious to keep in favour with his tutor.'

This could have been Brian talking and oddly enough the family concerned was called Johnston though they were not, as far as I can make out, related – at least not to their knowledge. On the other hand another old boy, while recalling – in the same book of public school history – that he had enjoyed his own Victorian schooldays, added that he 'knew nothing of what went on, except that I was starved and flogged, beaten and dirty'.

The dirtiness was still prevalent when Brian joined the school in 1925. As he later wrote, there were forty boys in his house, 'an absolute rabbit-warren' in Keats Lane, and there was just one proper bath between the lot of them. Boys were allowed a ten-minute soak once a week, and senior boys, known as KCBs or Knights Commander of the Bath, took it in turns to supervise the activity and make sure that the time was not exceeded. They also measured the depth of the water.

'Monty' used to go round the house every evening, chatting to his charges. If you were in the bath he had a habit of enquiring, 'What are you doing, little boy?'

When the boy answered that he was having a bath, Monty invariably commented, 'Lucky Dog!'

The only other means of washing was in a tin tub in one's room. Filling and emptying these was 'a particularly tricky job'.

These primitive arrangements sound too ridiculous to be

true, but even the official school history confirms that the place was in poor nick. In Brian's day ten new schoolrooms, thirteen fives courts and four squash courts were constructed. 'Nothing however was done to renovate the boarding houses, and Eton's main plant was becoming increasingly inadequate and in disrepair.' Even if de Montmorency had wanted to add on another bathroom or lavatory he would have had to make a formal application to the General Purpose Committee of the Provost and Fellows. On one occasion a parent offered £200 so that an extra lavatory could be installed in his son's house. The Committee turned the offer down.

After two years of de Montmorency's apparently unsatisfactory regime he finally retired and was succeeded by 'someone called Huson – rather a nice man, a bachelor'. According to de Walden the place then gradually became more civilised. In any case it hardly seemed to affect Brian. 'He was always joking, never stopped talking and always seemed to be laughing and enjoying life.' Brian became very fond of Huson, whom he regarded as being 'as near the perfect housemaster as one could get'. Huson had red hair, a purple face (he was supposed to have one less layer of skin than normal) and was something of a bon viveur. Often, after a heavy dinner, Huson used to repair to Brian's room, and lie on the floor in his evening dress doing keep-fit exercises. His favourite party trick was a hundred vertical leg raises without touching the ground. He died a decade or so later from a strangulated hernia which Brian always attributed to this eccentric post-prandial habit.

Although in some respects Eton resembled other 'public schools', the school was in other ways a place apart. It was by no means the oldest in Britain, indeed it was only founded in 1440, several hundred years after the earliest monastic schools in Canterbury and York. Of its two closest rivals, one, Winchester, was founded in the fourteenth century and the other, Harrow, just over a hundred years later, in the sixteenth.

Many other, older schools had greatly altered in character since the middle ages, whereas Eton seemed to have gone on largely unchanged, with a whole raft of esoteric customs and costumes, a unique school slang and games involving walls and fields which were played by nobody else in the world. In some ways it almost resembled a secret tribal society.

It was also a very grand society. When Lord Howard de Walden was beaten for looking as if he owned the place there was a certain rude justice in the remark, for his father, the eighth baron, was reputed to be one of the richest men in Britain, known as the uncrowned King of Wales. In Brian's last year at the school there were sixty-four peers or sons of peers among his contemporaries, and ten baronets. At the time of writing Eton has produced no fewer than eighteen Prime Ministers, one of whom, Sir Alec Douglas-Home, was the elder brother of Brian's greatest friend, the playwright, William.

'A wonderful club' was how Brian described it, adding that wherever he went in the world in later life he would bump into Old Etonians in important and influential positions so that having been at the school himself was 'extremely useful and has opened important doors'.

For not only do Etonians expect to inherit the earth – an expectation which is usually justified – they have a very highly developed sense of solidarity.

As the words of the famous school boating song has it:

Rugby may be more clever
Harrow may make more row;
But we'll row for ever,
Steady from stroke to bow;
And nothing in life shall sever
The chain that is round us now.

Although, unlike his father and brother, Brian was never a 'wet-bob', or rowing man, these were very much his own sentiments. Many of his closest friendships were entered into during these years, and although he had an enviable gift for making new friends all through his long life, it is the ones that he first found at Eton whom, I think, he valued most.

When reminiscing about school Brian seldom if ever talked or wrote about the academic side of life. He clearly performed well enough to satisfy his teachers and ultimately to gain a place at Oxford. But he never seems to have conceived any enthusiasm for study, even in areas where you might expect him to be interested – English language or literature for instance. Surprisingly, he was joint winner – with his friend Michael Branch – of the School Divinity Prize.

Even at this stage he had verbal fluency and a quickness of wit. Whether he also had academic gifts I am not so sure. I asked several of his oldest friends about this. Lord Howard de Walden said he thought he would rate 'about average', but when I asked Sir Edward Ford, he twinkled with amusement, and said, 'Oh rather below average I should say.'

I feel the jury is probably going to remain permanently out on the matter.

It was fun and games which preoccupied Brian most at Eton. Literally so. And, naturally, it was cricket which preoccupied him most of all. He records that each summer he progressed from one team to another, gaining his colours for

31

being one of the best twelve players in each age group. The names of the teams are wonderfully Etonian and arcane: 'Lower Sixpenny, Upper Sixpenny, Lower Club and Twenty-two.'

In 'Upper Sixpenny' his sense of humour almost cost him his place in the team. He was batting with a friend called Hopetoun who was on the fat side and consequently slow between the wickets. Brian hit the ball further than usual and started to run. By the time Hopetoun had turned to begin his second run Brian, always a speedy runner, had caught up with him and the two were running neck and neck towards the bowler's end. Brian overtook him swiftly and by the time he had run four Hopetoun was still only half-way through his third.

By this time the fielding side were all in stitches and the game effectively ground to a halt. Unfortunately for Brian the Captain of the XI had been watching from afar. Evidently he was most unamused.

In his last year Brian had hoped very much to play for the first XI, especially in the grand climax of the season against Harrow at Lord's. In those days this was an acme of the social and sporting season with Lord's packed out with horse-drawn carriages and the pupils of both schools decked out in top hats, tailcoats and the respective favours of the two establishments. Since Brian had made the grade at every age level up until now he had every reason to assume that he would make the team. However, he was foiled by a boy called Baerlein.

Baerlein, who came from a well-known sporting family, had already kept wicket for the XI for two years. According to Brian he should have left school since he was too old to stay on. Instead, wanting to play at Lord's for a third consecutive year, Baerlein behaved like a cad and a bounder, stayed on an extra half and thus deprived Brian of his rightful place in the team at Lord's.

Certainly this incident rankled with Brian and it bothered him throughout his life. Indeed it became one of his most often expressed public disappointments. He told the story so often that he and practically everyone else came to believe it. However William Douglas-Home, not for the first or only time, enters a cautionary note.

'I recall him saying once,' wrote Douglas-Home, 'that Baerlein (the elder brother of the racing correspondent) stayed on at Eton until he was twenty-seven (with a wife and seven children) thus excluding Brian from the first XI, of which Baerlein was the wicket-keeper. This, of course, was untrue, and Baerlein left Eton at precisely the same age as we did. But Brian delights in the thought of what, in his imagination, might have been.'

There is an element of mischief in this. Douglas-Home loved pulling Brian's leg, and at times it was a surprisingly easy one to pull.

Penelope Hatfield, the Eton College archivist, confirms that Baerlein did indeed stay on until an advanced age. He was born on 31 January 1912 and left at the end of the summer 'half' in 1931. So he was almost nineteen and a half by the time Eton played Harrow on 10 and 11 July. On the other hand, she writes, 'It is only fair to point out that Brian was only five months younger!' Baerlein, whose christian names were Anthony Max, arrived at Eton in 1925 so he was actually an exact contemporary of Brian's.

Brian's memory about Baerlein's performance 'behind the timbers' is a little less cloudy. The *Eton Chronicle*'s scribe wrote, 'Far too many balls were delivered down the leg-side, and of these far too many eluded the grasp of Baerlein, who must learn at all costs to be quicker on his feet. He took or neglected to take the leg ball again and again by a belated dive from his original position, so that he looked like a professional goal-keeper failing to save a penalty kick.'

Brian could be forgiven a mild chortle over that. Baerlein did not enjoy a particularly good season. He and Brian's friend, John Hogg, were described as being 'gravely out of conceit with themselves' – Eton-speak for suffering a temporary loss of form. In the second innings, however, he redeemed himself by taking two crucial catches, one very good. Eton won by an innings and sixteen runs.

A sad final coda to the story is that poor Baerlein was killed in action in 1941.

In any event the second XI was a much less pressurised team and the opportunity for fun correspondingly greater. Nevertheless the Eton and Harrow match at Lord's was a high point of the Season, not just for the schools concerned but for 'society' at large. At the match, the school coach, a great Yorkshire and England cricketer, George Hirst, adopted Brian for the duration, and led him all round Lord's, even taking him up to the scorer's box at the top of the grandstand, an exalted sanctum which Brian never again visited despite his long association with Lord's. He also spent much of the game in the Eton dressing-room eating cherries sent up for the occasion from Kent by Lord Harris, a famous cricketer in his day with Eton and England. So there were compensations.

The extent to which schools mark and define people is variable. Outsiders often think that Eton moulds its sons in a more obvious way than most. The phrase 'a typical Etonian' trips off many tongues with far greater certainty than 'a typical Harrovian' or 'a typical Wykehemist'. It has a pejorative ring and is associated with snobbishness, money, self-confidence (excessive), superiority and a la-de-da way of speaking. Several of those who knew him in later life said to me, quite forcefully, that Brian was never a typical Etonian.

He may well have 'talked posh' and he always seemed casually confident, but he never had a great deal of money and, without ever pretending to be anything other than he was, he was always utterly at ease with what he himself would have cheerfully described as 'other ranks'.

So, loyal though he was to his Alma Mater, I don't think you could describe him as 'typical'. Indeed in some ways he seems to have quite deliberately invented a one-off character for himself. Part of this was a cultivation of mannerisms and figures of speech which almost became trademarks throughout his life.

For example he would frequently announce himself with a trumpeting imitation of a huntsman's call to hounds. Years later his son Andrew remembers going with him to the BBC. As they walked through the front door Brian let out a loud 'Tantivy, tantivy' sound and continued it all down the corridor. As they walked along every office door flew open and there was a chorus of 'Hello, Brian', 'Good Morning Brian'. The habit dates from holidays around this time when, while living in Herefordshire, in one of a succession of rented houses, the Johnston children had a real hunting horn which they would blow. Sometimes, if lucky, the call would result in a real pack of hounds lolloping up the drive in response.

Another trick, this one learned from stepfather Scully, was folding up his enormous ears (three and a half inches from top to lobe) rather like one of those 'Pacamac', lightweight waterproofs which, turned inside out, form their own rucksack. When he grew much older he lost the knack of doing one ear but could manage the other and even demonstrated the trick when he appeared on television in *This Is Your Life*. Pauline Johnston was able to be precise about her husband's ear measurements because MCC needed them when planning their new museum. In it a life-sized model of Brian interviews a replica of W.G. Grace. Lord's said that if they had the right size ears, everything else could be reproduced to scale.

And there were verbal mannerisms too. They became lifelong catchphrases. At a Women's Institute Concert – or so he said – one of the Eton masters' wives sat through a particularly strangulated recitation of a French poem and finally turned to her neighbour with the words, 'Beautifully spoken, and how wise not to attempt the French accent.' The phrase became a sort of family joke in later years, so much so that at home he had only to say 'How wise . . .' for everybody to fall about laughing.

Another such phrase stemmed from tea with 'M'Dame'. The Eton house Dame was, in his own words, 'a sort of super matron, substitute-mother, state-registered nurse and catering expert all rolled into one'. Dames acted as a buffer between the boys and the housemaster and the 'library' of seniors who ran the house; and they were, on the one hand, figures of mild fun but, on the other, 'respected and loved'. Every term every boy in the house had a formal afternoon tea with M'Dame. Out of this ritual arose the sentence, 'Very good but very old – just like M'Dame's cakes.' This could be applied equally to things or people. Again Brian went on using it for the rest of his life.

The goal of most Etonians is membership of 'Pop'. This is the Eton Society, founded in 1811, as a debating club, though it stopped debating around the time that Brian was at the school. It was and is a self-elective élite. The writer Cyril

Connolly describes their distinctive uniform of 'bright coloured waistcoats, rolled umbrellas, buttonholes, braid and "spongebag" trousers'. Jo Grimond, the Liberal leader, who was a year Brian's junior, wrote of Pop:

'It is often in danger of being ridiculous, it is sometimes offensive and often useless, but always picturesque. Once having reached its haven boys, though assailed by many temptations, do at least become pleasant; and its very excellence lies in the fact that it is open to every danger and could never have originated in the brain of a schoolmaster.' It was, in the words of the school history, 'the effective boy authority'. Everybody aspired to membership and elections were bitterly contested. Many candidates were blackballed and the qualifications were ill-defined.

Brian became a member of Pop, though oddly, in his reminiscences about schooldays he seldom mentions the fact. For many Etonians it is the acme of their existence. Years later, he and his friends staged a number of reunions, first at the Savoy Hotel, later at the house of his friend Charles Villiers. His Pop friends were friends for life.

From Eton Brian passed without apparent effort to the University of Oxford, entering New College, where his father had been before him. An astonishing fifty-seven per cent of all Etonians went on to Oxford and Cambridge in Brian's time, and as the official Eton historian remarks, 'Those who went to University were not always the cleverest, and it is remarkable that Colleges were prepared to accept so many.'

Brian was certainly not the cleverest nor the most industrious but he was an Etonian, a member of Pop, and a useful wicket-keeper as well as being a wag. In those days that was more than enough. He would make a good all-round college man.

5

Not as New as All That
A Card at Oxford

New College, Oxford, is actually a good deal older than Eton.
It was founded by William of Wykeham, Bishop of Winchester in the latter half of the fourteenth century. Wykeham's
original idea was that it should operate in tandem with the
school he founded in Winchester in 1382 and throughout its
history the Oxford college has always contained a dispropor-
tionate number of scholars from the Hampshire public
school. This was certainly true in Brian's day, but apart from
the Wykehamists there were also twenty or so Etonians – not
nearly as bright as the Wykehamists – and quite a large
leavening of Rhodes Scholars from various Commonwealth
countries.

Jo Grimond, who went up from Eton to Oxford a year later
than Brian, in 1932, remarked once that 'in many ways Eton
must be the public school most like a university. Yet the
change from school to university seemed to me vast.'

For Brian the change seems to have been effectively
imperceptible. He carried on at Oxford, where he read
History, almost exactly as he had left off at Eton. He did the

39

mimimum amount of work necessary (in later life he doubted whether he could ever have really passed the New College entrance exam and put his success down entirely to the family connection); he played a lot of games, particularly cricket; and he cultivated his friendships while working hard on all-round fun with particular reference to practical jokes.

In fact he had not been particularly keen on going to university, but as the only real alternative seemed to be to enter the family coffee business, the sensible purple-faced Huson had been able to persuade him that university was a better option. Huson told him that he would not only enjoy himself but would also have the opportunity to learn about sex and drink as well as how to mix with people from all walks of life – something which was definitely not true of Eton. Since practically all his close friends at Oxford were men who had been at school with him, this last seems to have been a false prediction.

His main tutor was Wickham Legge, who had a curious laugh and whom Brian seems to have remembered chiefly for an unintended *double entendre* while discussing Henry VIII and his propensity to fever. Wickham Legge told his tutorial that 'Personally if I am in bed with a fever I toss off everything within reach.' This, needless to say, caused a great deal of mirth.

Brian claimed that he not only studied the books recommended by his tutors, and wrote a weekly essay but also 'averaged one lecture a day'. I have some doubts about this, especially as he says he was playing cricket 'at least four times a week – for his college team, the Oxford Authentics, Eton Ramblers and I Zingari. To compensate for this, he and various others went to a crammer during their last year called 'Mr Young's'. Mr Young gave them a crash course in the salient aspects of each period of history with which they were dealing and told them to work them into their exam papers no matter what the question. There were some bloomers, as when Young was discussing Anglo-Saxon agriculture and told his pupils about the 'fyrd'. Brian thought he said 'third' and when it came doing to writing the exam actually wrote about 'The Anglo-Saxon third'. This was remarked upon at his viva and caused him some embarrassment. However, he still managed a third-class degree. This is one better than his friend William Douglas-Home, who got a fourth, quite apart from twice being rusticated – once for being caught climbing into college, and once for going to a dance in London and leaving his bed unoccupied. The colleges in those days had very strict curfews and rules about always getting a good night's sleep in your own bed.

Brian, however, had no trouble about climbing into college because one day early on he observed the coalman delivering sacks to a cellar with its own separate door into college. He also saw that the coalman left the key in the lock. So, seizing his opportunity, he got a bar of soap, made an impression of the key while the coalman's back was turned and had his own key cut. From then on he was able to enjoy unrestricted access to New College at all hours of day and night.

As at Eton, he had failed to achieve the success he coveted at cricket. At New College he captained the college team two years running and on one occasion, according to him, the university captain played in a college match so that he could assess his form. There was apparently a chance that the incumbent wicket-keeper, P. C. Oldfield, might be unavailable because of pressure of work. (This sounds an unlikely story in those days!) Surviving contemporaries say that although he was unlucky to miss playing for the Eton XI, he really wasn't good enough to get a blue.

He also played rugger at Oxford and enjoyed two rare and eccentric successes. One was when he found himself marking H. G. 'Tuppy' Owen Smith, a South African Rhodes Scholar who had played full-back for England. Although Owen Smith ran rings round Brian, whose tackling was always suspect, there was an enjoyable small revenge when the great man shaped up for a drop at goal and, instead of attempting a tackle, Brian snatched the ball from his hands. This was definitely not orthodox. However, unfortunately for Brian, Owen Smith managed a speedy retaliation, promptly tackling him to the muddy ground.

The other occasion was even odder. Brian had his shorts ripped off in a tackle, and while replacements were being sought from the pavilion a friend lent him a macintosh to, as he put it, 'cover my confusion'. As he was standing on the touchline his side won possession and the ball was passed swiftly down the line. Brian could not resist it. He streaked back on to the field, took the final pass at wing three-quarter and scored under the posts. The referee was apparently laughing so much that he couldn't blow the whistle and the try was allowed to stand. Brian doubted it was legal – not because of the unorthodox attire but because he had failed to signal his return to the field of play. Later he would often claim very firmly – and probably correctly – 'I am the only person *ever* to score a try in a macintosh.'

Brian was clubbable at Oxford. Indeed he was the sort of man one associates with clubs. As an adult he was never more at home than at MCC or Boodles. At Oxford his clubs were the Grid, or Gridiron, which was 'moderately exclusive'; Vincent's, which was sporty; and the Bullingdon, which was 'unashamedly upper crust'. Members of the latter dined in very elegant tailcoats with blue facings, but all three did 'schoolboy' lunches or dinners including such Johnston favourites as scrambled egg. This was a welcome alternative to eating in College Hall, where Brian and his cronies would sit together and throw straw place mats at High Table until the dean, Henderson, came down to remonstrate in his evidently thick German accent.

He continued to run foul of Dean Henderson from time to time, most notably when he and some friends tested out a new car and were picked up by the police while doing seventy-five miles an hour. The Dean, not keen on fast cars, summoned them for an explanation and asked how fast they had been travelling. As one man the miscreants replied that they had been doing thirty-seven miles an hour. The Dean whistled. 'Ach,' he said – according to Brian – 'if you go at such speeds you must expect to get into trouble.'

On another occasion, when there was a concert in New College Chapel, Brian disguised himself as a tramp and sat outside with a cloth cap on the pavement. He had taken down some hunting pictures from the walls of his room and surrounded himself with these, though I'm not entirely sure why. He always said that he was begging not selling. As soon as the concert was over and people started to emerge he began to tell a terrible tale of poverty and hordes of children to support. Some of his friends, mingling with the crowd, lobbed some coins into the cap to the accompaniment of sympathetic cries of 'I say', 'Poor fellow' and 'What a shame'. Before long the university proctor and two bowler-hatted bulldogs hove in sight and Brian beat a hasty reatreat. He had made five shillings or so. This was just the sort of jape or prank that he was to play in his early days with the BBC. And huge audiences often proved just as gullible as the New College concert-goers.

He enjoyed dressing up and affecting slightly ridiculous disguises. When William Douglas-Home lost his driving licence for parking his car in Merton Street without any sidelights, he hired a horse and phaeton, named the horse Lily after the Lady Mayor of Oxford, and engaged Brian. Douglas-Home goes into some detail regarding Brian's service as his groom in his highly entertaining autobiography *Half Term Report*.

'Brian,' he wrote, 'entered into the spirit of the affair. He bought a sawn-off top hat in the Churchillian style, he placed a wisp of straw in his mouth and tied his trousers round below the knee with twine, and then he brought the phaeton round to Merton Street.'

Their first excursion was to take Lily to buy an evening paper. This almost ended in disaster at Carfax, where the two undergraduates had the greatest difficulty in turning their vehicle round, causing a serious traffic jam and an unseemly argument with the policeman on point duty.

In due course, however, they grew more accomplished, went for sight-seeing drives in the surrounding countryside and travelled to lectures by horsepower.

'She became a familiar figure in Oxford. The police grew to love her; and inevitably, gave her precedence at cross-roads. Bus drivers passed the time of day with her. The Press photographed her and wrote articles about her. A retired Colonel, writing from the Cavalry Club in London, offered me the free use of the harness in his stables and congratulated me on restoring a custom which, in his opinion, should never have lapsed.'

They had style, those two. And the legend of Lily lived on.

Fifteen years later, Douglas-Home's father visited Oxford in his capacity as President of the Boys' Brigade. After his speech he was accosted by an old lady.

'Lord Home,' she said, 'I must ask you. How is Lily?'

'Very well thank you, when I last saw her,' replied his Lordship, thinking that she was asking after Lady Home, whose name was Lilian.

'I'm so glad,' said the old lady. 'I used to love seeing her spanking down the High Street, with her harness glinting in the sun.'

'At this,' concluded William, 'my father raised his eyebrows and passed on.'

Brian and William Douglas-Home obviously had a bad effect on each other. Even all these years on you can hear them giggling away and spurring each other on to yet further dares and jokes. There was one moderately incomprehensible one where they pretended to some horsey members of the Bullingdon that they too were avid horsemen and wanted a whole lot of inside stabling involving grooms and stables. This doesn't sound terribly funny and in fact they were rather embarrassed by it and apologised.

Towards the end of their time at the university, however, both men rode in the Bullingdon point-to-point. This was particularly gallant of Douglas-Home, who had scarcely been on horseback, whereas Brian, as a boy, had been hunting once or twice under the watchful eye of his stepfather, Marcus Scully, who was a keen rider to hounds, always dressed in immaculate hunting pink.

They didn't have their own horses, so they hired a couple for the occasion and took a couple of practice rides, though they were too nervous to try out any jumps. Douglas-Home's horse was a reliable, plodding black horse called Nero, whereas Brian had an altogether racier number, a bay named Tip Top, who was alleged to be the half-brother of the previous year's Derby winner, April 5th. There was a special race for New College members and this was the one for which they entered.

Most of Brian's friends were as bent on mischief as he was so before the race a number of them went round the bookies putting on large bets on Brian at the tops of their voices. The result was that Tip Top, with Mr B. A. Johnston up, began the race as third favourite.

The two friends were left for dead at the off and Douglas-Home's Nero very sensibly pulled up at the second fence. Brian and Tip-Top somehow got round the course in one piece, though Brian used to say that after the first jump he was leaning back so far that his head was practically hitting Tip Top's hindquarters. In the unsaddling enclosure there were some boos from those who had been conned into placing bets on the unlikely duo, but Brian's friends cheered their hero loudly.

There was also a humorous club founded by Brian and his coterie called the Allsorts, which took on all kinds of local clubs at every conceivable sort of game, mostly played in a frivolous manner. Before the beginning one or other of the Allsorts always assumed some form of VIP disguise and solemnly shook hands with both teams. One of their regular fixtures was against a team composed of waiters from the town hotels.

All good fun. Old Huson had been right when he told Brian he would have three wonderful years, though there is no compelling evidence that Brian learned anything very useful about sex, nor that he consorted with people from every walk of life.

46

On the other hand he did learn at least one lesson connected with alcohol. After dinner at Brasenose one night he over-indulged in port and made himself so ill that he never ever again touched a drop of the stuff. For all that apparent breezy insouciance there was a ruthless self-discipline when required, even in those early days.

6

Where the Nuts Come From

An Awful Lot of Coffee in Brazil

The question of what exactly Brian was going to 'do' could no longer be deferred. His three years at Oxford had been partly designed to defer this difficult decision. Now, at last, it had to be faced.

His old schoolfriend, Lord Howard de Walden, remembers one of those adolescent conversations about what they were going to do when they grew up. When de Walden said, perspicaciously, that Brian would be a broadcaster, if only because 'you talk even more than I do', Brian demurred. A touch morosely he said that there really was no alternative but to go into the family firm. That meant coffee and it meant Brazil.

At first I was slightly perplexed to learn this, for Brian, after all, had two elder brothers. Why did neither Michael nor Christopher go into coffee? I consulted Christopher on this point and he gave me what seemed a plausible answer. Michael, the eldest brother, suffered badly from asthma, and it was agreed that his health would not stand up to a spell in South America. Besides he was academically below par.

Christopher thinks now that he may have suffered from dyslexia or some form of word blindness. At the time, of course, such complaints were not recognised.

As for Christopher, he had since the earliest years displayed an absolute passion for horses. Also, like most reasonably intelligent people in the 1930s, he could see that some sort of war with Hitler was probable if not inevitable, and he wanted to be in the armed forces when it happened. This led, inexorably, to a strongly expressed desire to join the cavalry. It was therefore accepted within the family that, on graduating from New College, Christopher should be commissioned into the 14th/20th Hussars.

Which left Brian to revive the family tradition, which had temporarily lapsed, and go into coffee.

The family firm, E. Johnston and Co. Ltd, was founded by Brian's great-grandfather Edward, who went to Brazil to seek his fortune in 1821 at the tender age of seventeen. He was the third of the nine children of Francis Johnston, whom we first encountered at the beginning of this story, moving south from the traditional Johnston lands in the Scottish Borders. His portrait as a young man certainly doesn't suggest a swash-buckling South American adventurer. Clutching a top hat in one hand and a pair of gloves in the other, he has a fey, almost foppish look, with long sideboards, soft eyes, a gentle half-smile and just a hint of that magnificent and characteristic Johnston nose. (Though in truth I think the Jimmy Durante look comes from Brian's mother's family. His was, in effect, an Alt nose!)

Six years after arriving in Brazil Edward married Henriette Moke, the daughter of a Dutch doctor from Tijuca, just outside Rio de Janeiro. After serving with the Dutch army Dr

50

1. Fancy dress *c.*1916. Among the group are Brian (*standing, centre*) and his mother, Pleasance (*tall woman, behind and to his left*).

2. Little Offley House, Hertfordshire, where Brian was brought up.

3. Anne.

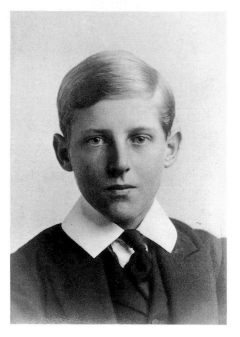

4. Michael.

The Johnston children *c.*1923–4.

5. Christopher.

6. Brian.

7. Wicket-keeper
Johnston (*middle row,
far left*) in the Temple
Grove First XI, 1923.

8. New boy at Eton,
1925.

9. Wicket-keeper extraordinary.

10. The Allsorts Club,
Oxford, played every
conceivable sport in
all manners of get-up.
(*Brian fourth from left in
middle row.*)

11. Running for
Oxford.

12. Brian nearly died of Acute Peripheral Neuritis while in Brazil. Sunbathing was prescribed as part of the cure.

13. The programme from Santos Athletic Club's production of Arnold Ridley's famous comedy *The Ghost Train*, in which Brian played the silly ass Deakin.

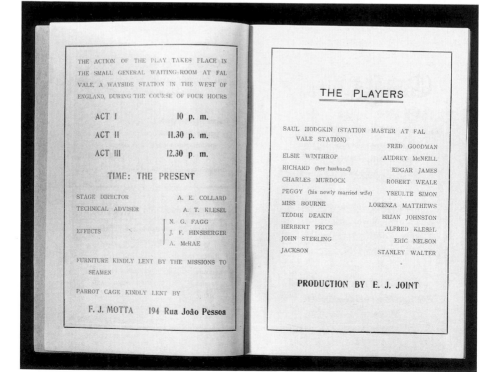

THE ACTION OF THE PLAY TAKES PLACE IN THE SMALL GENERAL WAITING-ROOM AT FAL VALE, A WAYSIDE STATION IN THE WEST OF ENGLAND, DURING THE COURSE OF FOUR HOURS

ACT I	10 p. m.
ACT II	11.30 p. m.
ACT III	12.30 p. m.

TIME: THE PRESENT

STAGE DIRECTOR	A. E. COLLARD
TECHNICAL ADVISER	A. T. KLESEL
EFFECTS	N. G. FAGG
	J. F. HINSBERGER
	A. McRAE

FURNITURE KINDLY LENT BY THE MISSIONS TO SEAMEN

PARROT CAGE KINDLY LENT BY

F. J. MOTTA   194 Rua João Pessoa

THE PLAYERS

SAUL HODGKIN (STATION MASTER AT FAL VALE STATION)	
	FRED GOODMAN
ELSIE WINTHROP	AUDREY McNEILL
RICHARD (her husband)	EDGAR JAMES
CHARLES MURDOCK	ROBERT WEALE
PEGGY (his newly married wife)	YSEULTE SIMON
MISS BOURNE	LORENZA MATTHEWS
TEDDIE DEAKIN	BRIAN JOHNSTON
HERBERT PRICE	ALFRED KLESEL
JOHN STERLING	ERIC NELSON
JACKSON	STANLEY WALTER

PRODUCTION BY E. J. JOINT

14. Entertaining the troops with Charles Villiers, October 1940.

15. The programme.

PROGRAMME

2ND. BN. GRENADIER GUARDS

PRESENT THEIR OWN

R E V U E

What about it then

DEVISED AND PRODUCED
BY
Brian Johnston
AND
Nick Allan

16. Near Thuine, Germany, in April 1945,
three weeks before the signing of the Armistice.

Moke had turned to business and acquired a considerable coffee plantation which, by the time Edward married his daughter, comprised at least a hundred thousand trees. He also indulged in some market gardening, specialising in asparagus and cauliflower.

When Edward Johnston first arrived Brazil was still a Portuguese colony. A year later the country became independent under the rule of the Emperor, Don Pedro I.

Slavery, which had been practised under Portuguese rule, remained a national institution. One visitor to Moke's *fazenda* remarked, approvingly, 'Some very nice outhouses are the dwellings of his blacks of whom he owns a good number and whose healthy, cheerful aspect, as well as their numerous lively children, speak of good treatment from their masters. In short, it is a perfectly arranged estate and it is rightly given the first place among all plantations in this country.'

Henriette Moke was, in other words, a very good catch. She was just nineteen years old when she married Edward Johnston, and he twenty-three.

At first Edward worked for a company called F. le Breton and Co., in Rio, rising to become joint manager in 1827. In 1831 he set up on his own account as an Exchange Broker. He seems to have prospered at this and in 1842, with two partners, established Edward Johnston and Co. in the Rua do Sabao, Rio de Janeiro. The infant firm had an interest in coffee from the first but also imported a wide variety of goods including cod, flour, wine, Swedish and American timber, salt, coal and iron.

Edward did not stay in Brazil for long after founding the firm which bore his name. Three years later he settled in Liverpool and, together with new partners, expanded the company greatly. In the mid-nineteenth century they were established in New York and New Orleans as well as Liverpool and South America.

As senior partner Edward, in the words of the company historian, 'dominated its affairs through his sons whom he moved about on the wide board of his activities like a master of chess'.

Eventually the founder retired to Brighton, where he died in 1876, leaving the company in the hands of two of his sons, Charles and Reginald. Of these two Reginald, Brian's grandfather, was the dominant one and arguably the most successful of the family so far. Between 1908 and 1911 he was Governor of the Bank of England.

It was the two sons who, in 1881, opened a new office in Santos which was then emerging as the chief port in Brazil. Santos, an island port some sixty miles from São Paolo, rapidly became the centre of the Johnston company's activities. It was an unhealthy place in those days with a fearful reputation as a breeding ground for Yellow Fever. For years there was a wreck in the Cubatao River, whose entire crew had perished from the disease. When a replacement crew was flown out they too caught the fever and died. The Johnstons themselves were not immune. Bertram Johnston, a grandson of the founder, contracted 'Yellow Jack' and died of it in 1890. Two years later 1,642 people died from the fever, and this at a time when the town's entire population was only twenty thousand.

To protect the European crews of their vessels, the Johnstons built a quarantined barracks on the Ilha das Palmas. Later, when various sanitary improvements eradicated the fever, the island became a popular resort area known locally as 'Johnston's Island'.

The English office of the Johnston company was moved

from Liverpool to London in 1862. The premises in Great St Helen's in the City of London were relatively humble though 'pervaded with a solid and quiet dignity'. Until 1900 at least, there were no telephones, no typewriters and no women clerks. The Johnstons were naturally conservative. When a junior partner took larger and more modern offices in Old Broad Street his colleagues simply refused to move. When, in 1914, the need for larger premises was generally acknowledged they went just a few doors down the street to No. 6, known as 'Brazil House'. Only in 1922 did they move further afield to 20 King William Street, which is where, eventually, Brian joined them.

For years there was a curious dichotomy in the business. The Brazil end, which from around the end of the century came under the control of non-family directors, was highly speculative and based on correctly forecasting fluctuations in the coffee market and the Brazilian currency – both volatile. The London end simply passed on the Brazilian asking prices to the London market and accepted or declined according to the wishes of their prospective clients. This was an altogether more staid activity.

Luckily the Brazil operation, mainly thanks to a partner called Edward Greene, was astutely and enterprisingly conducted and the company's fortunes thrived.

Gradually the next generation of Johnstons took their place in the partnership. In 1904, for instance, Charles Evelyn Johnston became a partner. He was the son of Reginald, the grandson of the founder and, as we have already seen, the father of Brian.

Nevertheless the Johnston family fortunes were beginning to wane. In 1910 the enterprising Greene came back from Brazil. At his instigation a new company, the Brazilian

Warrant Co. Ltd, was floated with an initial capital of
£300,000 which was swiftly raised to an impressive
£750,000. Among various acquisitions the new company
bought Johnston's freehold property in Santos.

'Henceforward,' says the company history, a little eva-
sively, 'the fortunes of E. Johnston and Co. Ltd. became
increasingly entangled with the Brazilian Warrant Co., Ltd.'
This is another way of saying that, in what amounted to a
boardroom coup, Greene had won out.

The outbreak of war diluted the already dwindling
influence of the Johnston family still further. In 1914 Greene
became Managing Director and the two leading younger
Johnstons – Charles and his brother Geoffrey – went to war. A
year later Geoffrey was killed in France. In 1917 the Brazilian
Warrant Company formally purchased E. Johnston and Co.,
though the smaller company, now a subsidiary of the larger,
continued to trade under its own name.

In the early twenties there was an almost total collapse of
the Brazilian economy, partly due to there being huge unsold
stocks of coffee in the country. As a result three London banks,
Barings, Rothschilds and Schroders came to the rescue with a
£9 million Brazilian Coffee Security Loan on four and a half
million bags of the stuff. Johnstons, where Brian's father,
Colonel Charles, was back in business, won the contract and
earned the fulsome thanks of the banks by managing the
entire sale successfully over a period of two years.

Then, in 1922, came Colonel Charles' sudden and tragic
death. A few weeks later Brian's grandfather Reginald, deeply
shocked, also died, so that the only member of the family
actively engaged in the affairs of the company was Brian's
uncle Francis. Alas, he only retained a formal connection with
the company for another three years.

So when Brian finally joined the staff in 1934 he was the first member of the family to be with the company for almost a decade. The misgivings he had expressed to Lord Howard de Walden at Eton were genuine and heartfelt. He would rather have done almost anything else than become a coffee-dealer. He toyed with teaching – he would surely have made a brilliant prep school head – and with acting, but in the end he joined the Brazilian Warrant.

For a year he worked in the King William Street office, commuting in by tube from South Kensington sporting the regulation bowler hat and rolled umbrella of the 1930s city gent. The job was menial with a salary to match. In later life he recalled learning to type with one finger (the typewriter had by now made its appearance at the office), draft a contract and decode a cable. He was introduced to a new vocabulary involving such phrases as 'draft at ninety days' sight' and 'cash against documents less two and a half per cent'. This, he claimed, convincingly, never to have mastered.

He also learned to taste coffee, a process which sounds much like wine tasting. In his case it seems to have involved a lot of sipping and gurgling of very hot and unadulterated coffee followed by a hearty spit into a large spitoon. He confessed later that he 'learnt to nod my head wisely and pretend I knew which was good and which was bad'. He often gave the impression of being one of the best bluffers in the business, though he was also good at playing the silly ass. The truth probably lies somewhere between the two extremes.

However office life did at least provide him with one good line. Sometimes I feel his life was measured out in anecdotes so that the only reason for a particular experience or period was that it could have a good story extracted from it. This could then be honed down and polished up and added to the repertoire. The story from his days in the City was a simple example of Johnston cheekiness.

Arriving late one morning, Brian was chided by a senior member of staff.

'Mr Johnston,' he said, 'you should have been here at nine-thirty.'

'Why?' replied Brian, quick as a flash, 'what happened?'

He was still making people laugh with that exchange more than forty years later.

Although work was boring to a degree, he made up for it in his spare time. Home at first was in Queen's Gate, Kensington, where he stayed with a wealthy banker, Alex Johnston, who was his uncle and godfather too. Life here was in some ways a throw-back to childhood days at Little Offley House, for there was a substantial staff of butler, footman, housemaid, under-housemaid, 'tweeny', cook and chauffeur. These Johnstons had no children and seem to have enjoyed thoroughly spoiling Brian, who paid no rent but returned their hospitality by staying in once a week to make up a hand at bridge.

Typically he was quick to befriend the staff – in particular Targett the butler and Edward the footman. Brian used to go below stairs to watch Targett playing cribbage with a one-legged tailor who always unscrewed his wooden leg before play began and parked it under the table. Targett gave Brian tips for the horses, delivered not very *sotto voce*, as he handed round the dishes at meal-times. In later years Edward used to 'valet' for Brian and 'buttle' at the Johnstons' parties.

Cricket, inevitably, was a prime source of rest and recreation, and Brian along with such old friends as John Hogg and Jimmy Lane Fox, turned out regularly for the Eton Ramblers. There was a certain amount of horseplay on the field. Keeping wicket, Brian teased one pompous Army officer by first donning a false moustache and then, a few balls later, a pair of dark glasses and a false nose (it must have been a very big one!). This so disconcerted the batsman that he was soon out. A few years later he met the same man who complained that in a previous match against the Ramblers a 'young whipper-snapper' had assumed a number of supposedly humorous disguises. 'What a bloody silly thing to do,' said Brian, never keen on confrontation if it could be avoided.

But most of his pranks took place after stumps had been drawn. Once he injected toothpaste into the favourite chocolates of Edgar Baerlein, father of the boy who had kept him out of the Eton XI at Lord's. When the port and chocolates arrived, old Baerlein bit into the chocolates and carried on talking quite unabashed despite the fact that he was literally foaming at the mouth. After one game Brian tied some kippers on to the cylinder block of a car belonging to a team-mate called Gerald Best (alias Percy Pine Tree because he was very tall and was alleged to sway in the breeze). The resulting smoke and smell was so extraordinary that it excited a passing dog into trying to scratch his way under the bonnet.

But the most regular butt of these jokes seems to have been Colonel 'Buns' Cartwright, Secretary and later President of the Ramblers. Sometimes it was nothing more sophisticated than a 'Whoopee' cushion on the seat of the Colonel's dining-room chair. The connivance of a compliant hostess and butler was a prerequisite. Sometimes the joke was more inventive. When they were staying with the Lane Foxes in Yorkshire, Jimmy Lane Fox's mother, very much life and soul of the party, let it be known that Buns was in the habit of relieving himself in the chamber-pot under his bed every night. Accordingly Brian filled a pot with orange juice, sausages and

– a really revolting touch – vermicelli. Unfortunately Buns rose to the occasion and at breakfast the next morning made no allusion whatever to the contents of the pot even though everyone knew that he must have discovered it when taken short in the small hours of the morning.

This last was the version told me by Sir John Hogg. Brian's was that he used lime juice (Rose's no doubt) and loo paper rather than vermicelli. And he remembered that Colonel Cartwright had been warned that the maids had not had time to deal with his room in the wake of the previous occupant. On discovering the pot, Buns, according to Brian, brought it downstairs and charged round the house showering everyone in sight with the contents.

Clearly there is a discrepancy here, and because so many of the principals – Brian, Buns and the Lane Foxes – are dead there is no way of pinpointing the exact historical truth.

Perhaps this doesn't much matter, though I prefer the Hogg version on the grounds that it makes Colonel Cartwright seem rather more stylish. The point is that Brian's humour, and, to be fair, that of his friends, was often profoundly lavatorial. It would be prissy and prudish to make too much of this, for in some ways it was just symptomatic of his times. Yet it is worth observing that if a similar exercise had been carried out in the late 1900s by a group of state-educated football fans it would have excited almost universal distaste. Old Etonian pleasures of the day were often vulgar, and by modern standards childish. And very politically incorrect!

The same could be said about music hall comedy, which became one of Brian's abiding loves. Now that he was a carefree bachelor based in London he loved nothing more than taking himself off, frequently alone, to have a simple supper while watching the popular comedians of the day perform. His haunts were the Palladium, the Holborn Empire, the Victoria Palace and the Chelsea Palace, and his heroes were Billy Bennett ('Queen Mary's favourite'), Randolph Sutton ('used to sing "On Mother Kelly's Doorstep" with tremendous pathos'), Nellie Wallace, Layton and Johnstone, the Western Brothers, the Crazy Gang and, perhaps above all, Max Miller.

Lovers of Brian's jokes and his style of word-play will realise immediately that these solitary evenings taught him at least as much as Temple Grove, Eton or Oxford.

Bud Flanagan, for instance, did a double act with his partner, Chesney Allen, in which he got all the place names inventively wrong. Thus King's Cross became 'His Majesty's Annoyed'. This was the sort of idiotic verbal ingenuity which Brian adored. A sort of crossword puzzle answer with jokes. And he loved anything a little bit naughty. Not actually blue. Many years later he seemed quite at ease discussing Bangkok massage parlours with his son. But what he really enjoyed were gags like this conversation between Flanagan and Allen:

Flanagan: I've been up to Scotland, where all the Scotsmen were wearing kilts.
Allen: Did you see the Trossachs?
Flanagan: No, it wasn't windy.
Both: Oi!

The final 'Oi' was mandatory in Flanagan and Allen sketches. Brian himself never quite emulated it, but he did often commit the cardinal sin of laughing at his own jokes. Being Brian, however, he somehow got away with it.

Max Miller was probably his absolute favourite stand-up comic, not least because he was the most *risqué*. He also had the trick, later copied most effectively by Frankie Howerd, of pretending that any filth was entirely in the minds of his audience. He taught Brian a lot about the *double entendre*.

Thus: 'A young girl of twenty-one married an old man of eighty-five and on her first night she prayed "Oh Lord, make me as old as my husband." And even as she was praying she felt old age creeping up on her.'

A very Brian joke. The verbal equivalent of one of those Donald McGill saucy postcards he loved sending to his friends.

After his tiresome apprenticeship in the City, he was sent to the company's Hamburg office – Germany was an important market for Brazilian coffee. Their agent was a former U-boat captain, and his assistant an avid Nazi. The latter took Brian to hear Goering address a rally where Brian said he felt very conspicuous in his City suit. It was during this speech that Goering offered his audience the famous choice between guns and butter, whereupon the entire hall rose to its feet, gave the Hitler salute, and started chanting. Brian, sounding – as he no doubt looked – rather like Bertie Wooster, reported, 'Even I could tell the one word they were shouting was *not* butter.'

After another spell in London, punctuated by visits to various continental ports, he set sail for Santos in June 1936. He doesn't seem by his own account to have enjoyed the experience. He arrived in a thunderstorm, immediately trod in a dog's turd, couldn't tell one coffee bean from another nor taste any difference in various types of coffee. He was, on his own admission, hopeless and therefore 'never given any job with any authority or responsibility'.

Two items of company folklore or gossip, unrecorded by Brian himself, have survived the ages. One is that before leaving London Brian invested in a quantity of tap-dancing shoes. On arrival he issued these to members of staff and conducted a tap-dancing class during every mid-morning coffee break. This sounds entirely in character. Legend has it that as there was a dearth of suitable unmarried ladies in town and a number of European bachelors, Santos sported a large number of bordellos, and that Brian was an enthusiastic customer. This may be so, but my guess is that the principal attraction for him in such an establishment would have been the pianist. Although, if they provided the same sort of nursery food as the Grid or the Bullingdon, that would have appealed to him as well.

William Douglas-Home used to tell a story which slightly confirms this view. One night William and a friend were at the Bag o'Nails, a well-known London night-club. Brian was at home in their shared lodgings fast asleep, and as a rather Brian-like prank William and friend persuaded one of the club hostesses to come home and give their friend a pleasant surprise. The girl was duly inserted into Brian's bedroom. Fifteen minutes later William quietly poked his head round the door to find the girl sitting demurely on the end of the bed while Brian described the day's play in the England–Australia Test match, ball by ball.

There was one compensation for the basic dreariness of his life in Brazil and that was amateur theatricals. Curiously he seems never to have done any acting or revue work either at school or university, but now, spurred on by those evenings watching the Crazy Gang and Max Miller, he compered, produced and took part in cross-talk acts taken word for word from the Holborn Empire. I came across a faded programme for one of these in a desk drawer in his study in St John's Wood. *Nuts in May*, it is headed. 'A Revue in Two Acts produced at the Santos Athletic Club'. The titles of the sketches have a wonderful whiff of corn and nostalgia. One was called 'I've Got a Horse' and featured 'Mystery Man from Newmarket – Brian Johnston'. Another was 'Two Snaps, or Why Take a Camera on a Holiday. She – Jean McNair. He – Brian Johnston.'

It was in Santos too that he had had his only major acting role as the silly ass character in Arnold Ridley's famous play *The Ghost Train*. Unfortunately when his big moment came at the final denouement he only managed to utter the first two lines of his great soliloquy before drying up altogether. This was greeted with much laughter by the audience, who evidently thought it was part of the play.

There is a photograph of Brian in one of these theatrical evenings with a group of fellow thespians. He had always been something of a string bean, and school photographs show him looking boney and almost hollow-eyed. In the Santos snap, however, he looks like death warmed up.

This is pretty much what he was, for after eighteen months in Brazil he was stricken down with Acute Peripheral Neuritis. This began by causing virtually total paralysis, and it sounds almost as if he was within inches of becoming the second member of the family to die in South America. Luckily he was skilfully nursed back to health by a couple called Deighton. Jerry was a member of the firm and his wife, Dorothy, a qualified doctor. He also had the services of an efficient Brazilian doctor called D'Utra Vaz, who prescribed 'a diet of raw vegetables, lots of tomatoes, which I hate, daily injections in the bottom and sunbathing'.

It was so serious that his mother came out to Santos to collect him and bring him back to England for convalescence. The family theory was that the disease was brought on by a chronic aversion to 'filthy foreign vegetables'. I consulted medical opinion (my own GP, a leg spin bowler and fervent Brian fan), and he confirmed that this was only too likely. Brian almost certainly hadn't been eating properly. In later life, characteristically, Brian made a joke of his illness. He used to say that it was normally brought on by pregnancy or an excess of gin – and neither was applicable in his case. At the time, however, there was nothing funny about it at all. Friends who remember his convalescence say that for a while he was seriously depressed.

After a short spell being fussed over by his rich relations in Queen's Gate he moved to 35 South Eaton Place, where he shared rooms with William Douglas-Home and they were looked after by 'a remarkable couple' called Mr and Mrs Crisp, also known as Gert and Crippen. All his life Brian had a great gift for finding 'remarkable' people to take care of him. Perhaps this was partly because he was generous and kind, not least to 'staff', but also because that little boy aspect to his character brought out people's paternal and maternal instincts. This is a guess but not, I think, a wild one.

Despite the imminence of war, the summer of 1938 was a halcyon period for Brian. His mother had divorced Scully and moved to a thatched cottage at Chearsley in north Buckinghamshire. Brian visited her there as often as he could. He went to the theatre and music hall. He stayed with friends, including the Homes in Scotland, where he impersonated a batty clergyman and put his hand on the knee of William's aunt before inviting her to join him outside in the shrubbery. William's uncle was unamused. That summer the Australians toured, and Brian got himself to Lord's for the second Test, where Hammond played 'one of the great Test innings of all time'.

By October he was fit enough to return to work. He was

promoted to Assistant Manager, on £500 a year, and given his own office together with a huge desk which had once belonged to his grandfather Reginald, the one who had governed the Bank of England.

It was not for him. He hated it. His flat-mate, William Douglas-Home, was acting in the West End and getting his plays put on there as well. When Brian consulted a fortune-teller she told him he was destined for a career in the entertainment world and would one day be famous.

But still he stayed safely, if glumly, behind his grandfather's desk. There, if it had not been for Herr Hitler, he might have remained for the rest of his life. That, luckily for him, and for us, was not to be. The crucial watershed in his life was fast approaching, and before long he was able to abandon any pretence of being a conventional everyday businessman and revel unashamedly in the role of being himself, an extraordinary and unique character and, by and large, one of his own peculiar invention.

7

Sound under Pressure

A Gallant Grenadier

His war started, in a fashion, some time before the formal outbreak of hostilities. After the invasion of Czechoslovakia in March 1939 it was clear that the rest of Europe was also on Hitler's agenda, and at one of the regular Old Etonian City lunches Brian and a group of friends had decided to join up as reservists.

With his view that life was all a series of interlocking networks, many of which involved Eton and his own family, Brian naturally decided to make good use of any such connection. It was also characteristic that he should aim for the top.

There was a happy coincidence here because his first cousin was a colonel of infantry called 'Boy' Browning, later famous as General Sir Frederick Browning, the creator and commander of the 1st Airborne Division. In the film *The Longest Day* he was played by Dirk Bogarde, who was widely thought to make him too effete. Johnston's fellow Grenadier, Lord Carrington, told me that Browning was 'absolutely terrifying'. Fifty years after serving with him, Carrington positively winced at the memory. Browning was also the husband of the novelist Daphne du Maurier.

In the late 1930s Browning was commanding the 2nd Battalion Grenadier Guards. They had recently returned from a two-year tour of Egypt and were stationed at Wellington Barracks. Brian and his chums were duly taken on as reservists and asked to present themselves at the officers' mess one evening in order formally to make the acquaintance of their commanding officer.

The chaps had arrived in their bowler hats, stiff white collars and dark suits, each man carrying a regulation rolled umbrella. Life seemed immensely agreeable as they lolled in leather armchairs and enjoyed a couple of leisurely drinks with the CO. Years later Brian recalled thinking at this moment what a great institution the Army was and what a civilised existence its officers led.

After a while Browning smiled silkily and said that he was sure they would like to meet the regimental sergeant-major who was even now awaiting their attendance. Johnston and friends ambled outside only to be met by the inimitable battle cry of a Guards RSM in full flight. Brian's memory was that RSM Tom Garnett ('wonderful man and soldier with whom I was to serve for most of the war') told them that they were a 'lazy lot of so-and-sos'. His language was almost certainly a deal saltier than that, but in any event he had the young gentlemen doubling up and down the square for twenty agonising and quite unexpected minutes before they were dismissed with a 'Good-night, gentlemen, see you later in the week' and allowed to drip back into the mess for a further restorative snifter and a lecture from Browning on drill and discipline in the Brigade of Guards, vital importance of.

In the years to come Brian became an intensely loyal and

66

proud Grenadier, even if he never quite conformed to the well-drilled conventions that Browning talked about in that inaugural chat. Mind you, Browning was no slave to convention himself. Some years earlier he had been on parade at Sandhurst on horseback as adjutant. Towards the end of the ceremony it began to rain and Browning, who was fanatical about his kit and turn-out, was determined not to get wet. Instead of riding off in the normal manner he decided the nearest shelter was the front entrance of the Royal Military College, and so he promptly rode his horse up the front steps. This was considered so stylish that it established a tradition, and to this day adjutants at the College always ride their white horses up the steps at the close of the sovereign's parade.

One of his superior officers was Patrick Winnington, a regular soldier with a regular soldier's views. As such he admits that he was 'surprised at Brian's unorthodox, refreshing and unusual approach to the job'. It says much for the Grenadiers that they were able to accommodate such eccentricity and turn it to their advantage. Brian's nickname for Winnington was 'Floorboards' – a sobriquet which, like so many of the Johnston monikers, stuck with him for the rest of his life. Winnington's wife Betty objected to it strongly, however, and told Brian so on every occasion. I was unable at first to find out why he was called that, but Lord Carrington, 'The Small Peer', was able to cast light on the matter. 'Need you ask?' he said. 'We were in some God-awful camp in bell tents and the only one who had floorboards was Patrick Winnington!'

Until 1944, Brian's was something of a phoney war. When Chamberlain made the formal declaration of hostilities on 3 September 1939, he was filling sandbags outside the Westminster Hospital. Typically, he was more relieved than distressed that the months of hanging around appeared to be over, and he immediately began badgering regimental HQ asking to be taken on the strength.

Eventually he was summoned for the usual undignified and somewhat rudimentary medical examination. First came the naughty bit, where the doctor holds your testicles and says 'cough' – an excuse naturally for one of his wonderfully corny jokes (the one about 'the recruit who started to run as he thought the doctor said "off" instead of "cough". Very painful!') As for the bit where he was required to read letters with first the left and then the right eye, he very nearly failed. He managed the left perfectly satisfactorily but, being short-sighted in the right, was making heavy weather of this part of the exercise. The examining officer, seeing the problem, obligingly opened the fingers that he was using to cover Brian's left eye and the test was safely passed. In later years Brian habitually read with a hand over one eye.

In October he and his friends went down to Sandhurst as the first members – he described them as 'victims' – of the new war-time system. This involved a crash training course, an Officer Cadets Training Unit, which lasted only four months as against the more leisurely two years of peace-time. At first the 6 a. m. reveille and the endless drill and PT were a shock to his system, but before long he and his brother officers settled into comparative enjoyment. He found this period, the last months of 1939, 'a strange mixture of war and peace'.

Most of them were comparatively well-to-do. Not only did they tend to come from relatively affluent backgrounds, they were also mature men in their mid-twenties who had held down rewarding jobs for several years. Consequently most, including Brian himself, owned motor-cars. These were kept parked in down-town Camberley, nearby. On Saturdays, when those not on guard duty began a period of weekend leave, the cars were driven over to Sandhurst by chauffeurs so that the young officer-cadets could drive up to town for a little rest and recreation.

On the first Saturday they went out for a route march in the morning and when they returned to the parade ground they found that it had been transformed into a car park covered with their own jalopies. Some of the cars were ostentatiously grand. One friend of Brian's, Ken Thornton, recalling the incident, admits to a Rolls-Bentley.

One of his comrades at Sandhurst was Alfred Shaughnessy, some three years his junior, who had looked up to him as 'rather a swell' at Eton, played cricket with him at Lord Howard de Walden's Chirk Castle and was later to win fame and fortune as a playwright and scriptwriter, most notably for *Upstairs, Downstairs*.

Shaughnessy remembers the 'tremendous fun' of nights in the mess and particularly of 'Brian calling out "Come on, Alfred J., get on the keys!" and I used to play the piano, which I did often.' After the Guards Armoured Division landed in Normandy in 1944 there were countless parties in the mess. Shaughnessy always took to the keyboard and Brian always sang. The first favourite was 'Underneath the Arches' ('more or less his signature tune') which Shaughnessy reckons he played for Brian literally hundreds of times. The second was 'We'll gather lilacs in the spring again.'

'Very sentimental fellow, Brian,' says Shaughnessy. 'What is not entirely recognised is that behind that terrific jokey non-stop funny façade, that fast-talking comedian, was a very very sensitive, thoughtful man. Enormously kind. Never say a malicious word about anyone. He had the kindest heart and he was immensely sentimental. You only had to play a couple

69

of Noël Coward waltzes and his eyes would fill with tears. He loved show music, particularly when there was a good melody. He could sing a good many of them and knew the words pretty well. And occasionally when there was no one to play for him he would sit down at the piano and try to do "Underneath the Arches", which he had worked at and could *sort of* get through at a pinch.'

There was one particular Sandhurst incident involving Brian which Shaughnessy says he will never forget. From time to time cadets took it in turns to drill the company under the beady eye of an intimidating Coldstream drill sergeant called 'Dusty' Smith. One day Smith called out George Jellicoe to drill them. Jellicoe, son of the famous Admiral, had a head which was too big for the standard khaki 'fore and aft' cap, so by special dispensation of the Commandant he was allowed to wear the check cloth cap that he wore at home when out shooting. It looked most incongruous with khaki battle dress. He cut a less than prepossessing figure. 'He looked like a Red Chinese engineer,' says Shaughnessy.

Everything started conventionally. Jellicoe shouted 'Company, 'tenSHUN!' and the company came to attention. 'Then,' says Shaughnessy, 'he called "By the left, quick march!" and we all marched off across the lawns towards the lake, heading for the water like the Gadarene swine. After a while we vaguely heard poor old George in the distance screaming and yelling "Company, about turn!" and trying to stop us before we went too far.'

It was at this moment that Officer Cadet B. A. Johnston took over. 'Pretend we can't hear!' he said. 'Keep marching.'

And so the company marched on into the lake, where they halted and marked time with water splashing all over the place until a very angry bellowing drill sergeant came up to them at the double, turned them round and marched them back to where George Jellicoe was standing in his tweed cap with 'egg over his face'.

'Little did we realise,' says Shaughnessy, 'that within a very few years George would be First Lord of the Admiralty, Leader of the House of Lords and God knows what else.'

After Sandhurst Brian was posted to the Grenadiers' Training Battalion at Windsor which, at first, was much like Sandhurst, only with RSM 'Snapper' Robinson being substituted for CSM 'Dusty' Smith. After a few weeks, however, he was allowed to assume guard duty at the castle which, since Princess Elizabeth and Princess Margaret were at home there, did at last seem like part of a serious war effort.

In early May 1940 he was ordered to report to Wellington Barracks before joining the 2nd Battalion in France. Alas, this was not to be. The 2nd Battalion were bundled back to Dunkirk along with the rest of the British Expeditionary Force and were lucky to escape more or less intact though minus their kit. When Brian did finally join them they were licking their wounds in Shaftesbury, a sleepy old hill-top town in the north-eastern corner of Dorset.

Here the sociable, garrulous Brian had a bruising experience to which he reacted with unaccustomed vehemence. In a way this was out of character, because he was generally a stickler for convention and etiquette. The custom was that in the mess no one spoke to a newly joined officer except in the course of duty. Even old friends could appear to cut one dead. In peace-time this could go on for ages, but in war it lasted a fortnight. Brian was outraged. 'It made all those who took part,' he later wrote, 'look not only ridiculous but boorish and bad-mannered and I cannot believe that it did anyone any good.'

It certainly cut against his naturally gregarious grain. He took a quiet revenge in his autobiography by telling the story, almost certainly an apocryphal Johnston tale, about the newly joined officer whose CO said he'd soon settle down with his new battalion, especially after the heavy drinks session on Monday nights.

The new recruit said he didn't drink.

The CO looked a bit stony and said that in that case he'd enjoy Wednesdays, when they had a few local nurses, ATS, and other floosies in for a spot of slap and tickle.

The new recruit said he didn't approve of that either.

The Colonel was now quite seriously cross.

'Are you by any chance a queer?' he enquired.

'Certainly not, sir,' replied the new recruit.

'Pity,' said the Colonel, 'then you won't enjoy Saturday nights either!'

Naturally he settled in well after the silly first fortnight. Once the battalion had been given new kit they moved to Middleton-on-Sea where Brian, ever the aspiring music hall artist, had the huge thrill of seeing the pianist Charlie Kunz sunbathing outside his house. Then, soon afterwards, they transferred to Parkstone, Dorset. There he was put in charge of first the mortar platoon and then the motor-cycle platoon. As Brian tells it, he was a bit of a duffer on both counts. The motor-cycles had been bought off the general public second-hand and Brian was supposed to lead his platoon, in theory the spearhead of the crack 3rd Division, sitting in a side-car armed only with a revolver.

'I still cannot understand,' he wrote later, 'why Hitler never invaded.'

According to Brian the view was taken that he would never make a good front-line soldier so he was sent on a training course at Minehead with a view to becoming Transport Officer.

Then, in May 1941, he had what he described as 'two bits of news, one good, one bad'. The bad news was that 35 South Eaton Place had been demolished by an enemy land-mine. The Crisps had survived, fortunately, shaken but intact. The good news was that thereafter his London billet was the Savoy Hotel. The bonus was that his battalion was to be part of a new Guards Armoured Division. They would stop being poor bloody infantry and would have tanks instead. Brian was going to become a Technical Adjutant. He was certainly not of a technical bent, any more than his number two, Gordon Tozer, his future brother-in-law.

To prepare for this, he was sent on another training course, this time at Bovington (home now of the National Tank Museum). One of his fellow trainees was William Whitelaw, later the celebrated Tory grandee. Cue for Whitelaw's story, often told by both men. When I asked Lord Whitelaw about it, he said simply, 'You know the story. It's in all the books.'

As indeed it is.

Having compared the Whitelaw version with the Johnston one, it seems to me that although there are discrepancies this is more or less what happened. The two of them together, and likewise a rather older man, Gerald 'Daddy' Upjohn, were given an engine to dismantle and reassemble. Looking around the room where other men were charged with similar tasks, it became apparent that after reassembly there were always a few nuts and bolts left over. Taking the engine apart was easy. Putting it together again was altogether more difficult.

The inspecting officer asked each man to turn out his pockets, and if he found nuts and bolts which had not been re-incorporated he became extremely cross. Needless to say, both Whitelaw and Johnston had several nuts and bolts for which they could find no home. At Brian's suggestion they slipped them surreptitiously into Upjohn's pocket.

Thus, when the inspecting officer arrived and asked them to turn out their pockets, both Whitelaw and Johnston were 'clean' but the innocent Upjohn had a pocketful of redundant bits and pieces.

When the inspecting officer began to upbraid Upjohn the culprits confessed, but the matter was made worse, predictably, by William Douglas-Home, who had been watching the whole exercise with typically sardonic eye.

'Put these wicked officers in gaol,' he volunteered. 'They are very bad men.'

The inspecting officer in Johnston's version 'could not help laughing', though in Whitelaw's story he was 'fed up'. In any event the incident was closed except that in their final reports all three received the same verdict: 'These officers appear to be unsound under pressure.'

Lord Whitelaw thinks history proved otherwise and I'm bound to agree. 'Uppers' became Sir Gerald Upjohn and a High Court judge, and we all know what happened to Johnston and Whitelaw.

Back with the battalion at Warminster, Brian found himself in charge of a commandeered civilian garage and a staff of forty fitters. It was their job to maintain and repair some seventy-five tanks and over a hundred trucks and scout cars.

For some reason when they became an armoured battalion they all had to wear berets. Brian was certain that he would look ridiculous wearing one, so he formed up his forty fitters and told them that he was going to put on his new headgear and they could have a two-minute laugh. Once that was over he never wished to find anyone laughing at him. If he did they would be put under close arrest for insolence. As he said himself this was 'a bit unorthodox'. Nevertheless it seemed to work. In any case I'm not sure Brian would have looked any funnier than anyone else in a beret.

Brian's only war wounds were incurred on Salisbury Plain. Once his scout car ran into an old shell hole and the famous nose lost an argument with the armour plating. In his own words it was 'too big and too tough' to break but it needed a lot of stitches and he said that he bore the scars for the rest of his life. The other injury was even less glamorous. Lifting a heavy object – probably a tank track – he ruptured himself and had to have a hernia operation. Cue, typically, for a Johnston joke about a man having a rupturous time in a Truss House in Herne Bay.

There are times when one finds oneself echoing his future father-in-law's exasperation. Can't this man be serious about anything?!

From Warminster the battalion went to Norfolk, where they abandoned their old Covenanter and Crusader tanks and acquired the Shermans with which they were later to do real battle with the enemy. It was in Norfolk that he had a chance meeting with two men who were later to change his life. These were the Canadian war correspondent Stewart MacPherson and another broadcaster, Wynford Vaughan-Thomas, then attached to the Irish Guards. The two came over to Brian's battalion and enjoyed what Brian describes as 'an hilarious evening'. They obviously took a shine to Brian. Now, alas, both are dead, but I spoke to Stewart MacPherson on the telephone a few months before his death in April 1995. MacPherson told me that Brian was quite simply one of the funniest men he'd ever known. And he knew it immediately that evening in the Norfolk mess. A natural broadcaster recognised a soul-mate on sight.

From Norfolk they moved to Yorkshire for more exercises. Brian and his team acquired three white hens which they kept in the tool-box on top of the cab of the store truck. Thanks to their prowess at laying, Brian enjoyed regular fry-ups in the back of the truck.

Finally, in 1944, the battalion moved to Hove to prepare for the Normandy landings. Because of bad weather Brian's men didn't sail until some three weeks after the initial invasion. The voyage to Arromanches was remarkable for two minor disasters. The Guardsmen mistook the wash-basins on board their landing craft for urinals and accordingly urinated in them. This led to outrage in the Senior Service and to the sailors referring to the Guards as 'those pissing pongos'.

The three white hens had had to be abandoned, but not before two buckets full of their eggs had been pickled. These buckets were hung from the roof of the store truck. Unfortunately the sea was rough and they were unable to make the smooth beach landing they had anticipated. Instead the truck had to be driven down a steep ramp into the water. As a result the buckets swung violently and hurled eggs all over the place. Enough were salvaged to make a fry-up later that day in an orchard near Bayeux, but it was not an auspicious start.

The countryside of Normandy, the 'bocage' with its small fields, hedges and ditches and narrow lanes, was notoriously bad tank country. For some time the Division remained virtually immobile, acting as a sort of decoy for the Americans who were poised to attack the Germans at the Falaise Gap. On 18 July they had their first serious taste of battle, which Brian remembered as 'bloody and chaotic'.

His public reaction to tough fighting and heavy opposition which involved the loss of nine of the battalion's tanks, was generally typically laconic and understated: 'Not much fun.' That's slightly unfair. In his autobiography he did actually write a trenchant paragraph about those days of battle between June and October which gives a rare public glimpse of his deep feelings:

> The heat and the dust, the flattened corn fields, the
> 'liberated' villages which were just piles of rubble,
> the refugees, the stench of dead cows, our first
> shelling, real fear, the first casualties, friends
> wounded or killed, men with whom one had laughed
> and joked the evening before, lying burned beside
> their knocked-out tank. No, war is *not* fun, though as
> years go by, one tends to remember only the good
> things. The changes are so sudden. One moment
> boredom or laughter, the next, action and death. So
> it was with us.

Then suddenly they got what he described as 'a green light' and set off at high speed across France and Belgium. The battalion covered 395 miles in a week and did 93 miles in a final day, ending up as the liberators of Brussels. It was a bitter-sweet episode. One minute it was flowers and bunting and pretty girls who even kissed the Technical Adjutant. The next moment one would come round a corner and find one of the battalion's Shermans burned out with one's fellow Guardsmen lying dead beside it.

His number two, Gordon Tozer, acquired a girl-friend in Brussels. Brian manfully covered for him when he went on clandestine trysts. He also managed to get his hands on a secret store of vintage Krug champagne abandoned by the Germans. This was stored in one of his petrol lorries and handed out to the tanks along with supplies of more orthodox fuel.

Two weeks later the battalion took the Nijmegen Bridge, where they linked up with Airborne troops under the command of Brian's cousin 'Boy' Browning, who, of course, had formerly been commander of this very battalion. A poignant moment. The successful assault was led by his friend 'The Small Peer', Peter Carrington.

As history knows, the war was prolonged for many cold and brutal months. No fun at all. During this period, however, 'on the lighter side', Brian actually captured some enemy soldiers. One evening he was steaming along in his scout car to rescue some tanks in a burning village when he saw three German soldiers rise up out of a ditch and advance towards the car. Prudently he pulled down his armoured hatch and retreated to relative safety. The next thing he heard was banging on the side of his vehicle and voices calling out 'Kamerad!' Peering out through the visor he saw that the enemy had their arms raised in surrender. By his own account Brian then became a true Grenadier, ordered the Germans on to the car and bore his prisoners home in triumph.

On 26 April the Division captured Bremen. Hamburg fell on 2 May and three days later the Armistice was signed. Now that the war was over the Guards were to revert to their former traditional role as infantry. On 9 June there was a grand final parade of three hundred tanks in front of Field Marshal Montgomery. Monty was gratifyingly complimentary.

Towards the end of the war Brian was awarded the Military Cross. This coveted medal is, in effect, a sort of cadet version of the Victoria Cross, traditionally awarded to young officers for acts of particular gallantry. Brian, with typical self-deprecation, always used to maintain that it was 'handed out with the rations'.

This I simply do not believe. The fellow Grenadiers who had served with him all testified to his bravery and, in particular, to his morale-boosting qualities. There was no more cheering sight when your tank became incapacitated within range of enemy gun-fire than Captain Johnston in his scout car cracking terrible jokes about Jerries and calling up expert relief from his technical staff. His vehicle had the acronym 'FUJIAR' stencilled on the side, standing, of course, for 'F*** you Jack, I'm all right!'

His old friend Freddie Shaughnessy was coincidentally Brian's oppo, serving as Technical Officer in another of the Guards' Armoured Battalions. He told me something which Brian never seems to have mentioned – that their Sherman tanks were irreverently known as 'Tommy Cookers' because they invariably ignited when hit by enemy fire. Part of the Technical Adjutant's job was the hideous one of physically pulling badly burned and burning Guardsmen from their stricken vehicles.

Brian's citation, in the typical clipped military style of the day, reads as follows:

> This officer has been Technical Adjutant of the
> Battalion under my command since the Bn landed in
> France and, as such, has been responsible for the
> mechanical efficiency of the Bn. The outstanding
> results attained have been due to his energy, powers
> of organisation, and ability to inspire his staff of

fitters, as well as by his own mechanical knowledge and capabilities.

Since crossing the Rhine and advancing through waterlogged country, he has had the task not only of recovering tank battle casualties, often under fire, but also 'unbogging' a great many tanks. Often, had it not been for the efficiency with which this officer has recovered tanks, squadrons would *not* have been able to have gone into battle.

His own dynamic personality, coupled with his untiring determination and cheerfulness under fire, have inspired those around him always to reach the highest standard of efficiency.

This is a fine testimonial which carries the ring of truth, and yet it is not what I associate with the Military Cross. My father also had a Military Cross, and his citation refers to a few relatively brief moments at the landing in Salerno when he was engaged in ferocious hand-to-hand fighting. My sense was that this decoration was usually awarded for just such flashes of glory, not for sustained achievement over a long period.

His friend William Douglas-Home, who spent much of his war in prison for disobeying an order – it involved indiscriminate shelling of Le Havre and would have resulted in the death of many innocent civilians – quizzed Brian about his award.

At first Brian refused to tell him but finally said, 'All right, I'll tell you if you really want to know, you nosey bugger.'

Douglas-Home's story is that Brian recited the first line of his citation, inventing some stuff about attacking the enemy with 'cold steel'.

Douglas-Home remonstrated in typically bantering manner by pointing out that as Technical Adjutant in a tank regiment the only cold steel Brian would had access to would have been a spanner.

Brian agreed.

'Then why did your colonel write such a thing?'

'He didn't.'

'Who did then?'

'Me,' said Brian.

Douglas-Home was wryly caustic about this – as was his wont. 'There the matter rests,' he wrote, 'and there on Brian's chest at regimental dinners and the like, the medal rests as well. Never mind who composed the citation, one can be quite sure that it was well earned.'

Pauline was puzzled that I was puzzled, sensing, I think, that I was questioning Brian's right to the award. I wasn't doing that but I was definitely curious.

I am not an expert, however, so I consulted John Keegan, the former Sandhurst lecturer who is now Defence Correspondent of the *Daily Telegraph* and one of our leading military historians.

Keegan concurred but offered an explanation. 'I agree,' he wrote, 'that the citation is surprising in tone. However MCs are – also to my surprise – given for cumulative achievement rather than specific acts in many cases.'

Keegan's theory is this. 'Since the end of the war was approaching, I suspect that his commanding officer took the view that Johnners had been a thoroughly good officer who deserved a medal and that he had better get the citation in sharpish before peace supervened. Moreover battalions tended to be allotted a share of medals to be awarded at the CO's discretion.'

Keegan adds, a touch waggishly, that 'The Foot Guards were very good at seeing that their officers and soldiers were decorated.'

Without in any way diminishing the excellenece of the Johnston war record, this does go part of the way to explaining what Brian meant when he said that his gong had been handed out with the rations.

He always disclaimed any great technical ability. Pauline told me that in later years, though generally no dab hand at do-it-yourself or even plug-changing, he always seemed to know what was going on under the bonnet of a car. Although the famous Willie Whitelaw story carries the ring of truth I suspect it has been slightly embellished over the years. And Brian was incorrigibly self-deprecating. He might not have been able to roll his sleeves up and deal with plugs, gaskets or widgets, but he would have been more than capable of diagnosing the problem and calling up the relevant expert. That was his role – he and Gordon Tozer were GPs, not brain surgeons.

More important than that he was, as he had been in his early years and as he was later to be on difficult foreign tours and in potentially bickering commentary boxes, the supreme morale booster and lifter of flagging spirits.

As General Sir David Fraser has written, it was not his professional competence that won him his MC, it was his extraordinary personality:

> He was renowned throughout the Guards Armoured
> Division. Irreverent, gallant, irrepressible,
> impertinent to the exalted in a way which every
> recipient of the impertinence enjoyed, chuckling
> whatever the circumstances, cracking appalling jokes

however hellish the war or the weather, Brian probably did more than any other human being to maintain morale in any circumstances, to encourage, cheer and induce laughter in soldiers however dark the day. He was widely and deservedly loved and among his own men in the technical department he was a being entirely unique. It was impossible to mention his name to anybody, in any context, without an answering grin.

Patrick Winnington, who had been on the staff but returned to Brian's battalion as second-in-command after the liberation of Brussels, provides a further personal gloss.

All his staff had nicknames [he told me], and it often happened that one would hear his familiar voice on the radio from his scout car – 'There are two tanks at Map Ref . . . which are broken down and another wants repairs to the tanks. Please tell "Gandhi" and "Burglar Bill". Also I would like to see "Honest Joe" when I get back to Battalion HQ.' Brian earned his MC for the fearless and efficient way he organised the recovery of vehicles and tanks in the battlefield, often under fire.

After the fighting had ceased and the Battalion HQ was housed in a very fine *Schloss* near the Rhine at Siegberg, Brian and I shared a room the size of a small ballroom. As you can imagine there was never a dull moment. But anyone who thinks that Brian was just a buffoon would be entirely wrong. He was extremely intelligent, a very caring and charming person who knew exactly when it was necessary to be serious. Underneath all the badinage he was very efficient and, most important, no one ever heard him say an unkind word about anyone. In my experience of life that is very rare indeed and illustrates what a very nice person Brian was.

He adds that at this time 'Brian found himself having to organise concerts and entertainments, which of course he did brilliantly.' There was no question of Brian 'having' to organise them. Wild horses couldn't have dragged him away from them.

He had already put on several evenings in England while the Division was still preparing for the Normandy landings. His collaborator then had been his fellow Technical Adjutant 'Alfred J'.

After the war was over and he was holed up in the Rhineside *Schloss*, he and Shaughnessy put together a victory revue called *The Eyes Have It*, an eye being the Divisional logo.

'It was all based around Brian,' says Shaughnessy. 'He was the centre-piece because he had this wonderful technique of the stand-up comedian, all modelled on Max Miller. He could just stand up on stage and rattle off these terribly funny one-liners, and jokes just like machine-gun-fire one after the other. Which of course he did with great skill to his dying day.

'Like his God, Max Miller, he could be rather blue at times.'

Somehow he managed to tell the blue numbers without being particularly offensive. Shaughnessy puts it down to Brian's inherent charm. It also has something to do with the fact that the jokes themselves have the innocence of a bygone age, rather like the saucy picture postcards he so enjoyed. To a post-Lenny Bruce generation they really don't qualify as 'blue' at all.

Even so there was one occasion when Brian misjudged part of his audience. During the run of *The Eyes Have It* he told the story about the honeymoon couple cycling on a bicycle made for two.

They arrive at the bottom of a steep hill and the boy says to the girl, 'This is where we get off and I push it up.'

To which she says, 'That's fine, but what do we do about the bike?'

A good old joke which served Brian well over most of his life. And pretty harmless. It normally gets a biggish laugh but on one occasion in 1945 it elicited a considerable clatter from the back of the hall. Alfred J. remembers it well: 'Seven or eight very angry uniformed ladies, colonels and commandants from the ATS and various other women's armed services rose from their seats like icebergs and marched from the back of the hall in a rather pointed way. Well, after a brief consultation Brian and I decided that the gag should stay in the show until the end of the run, and it did.'

Another lighter wartime moment which the two men always remembered was from the earlier days of training in the UK, at a place called Duncombe Park in Yorkshire. Shaughnessy wrote a revue called *It's All (L)aid On*, in which at one moment they had a young guardsman called O'Brien with a fine tenor voice playing a prisoner of war and singing an Ivor Novello song called 'Shine Through my Dreams' from *Glamorous Night*.

He played the part with a garland of barbed wire and a cardboard watchtower in the background. It was all very affecting, says Shaughnessy, and there wasn't a dry eye in the house. One night, however, they had a temporary stage manager called Hugh Burge who tried to wrap the scene in too much of a hurry and got entangled backstage in the barbed wire. 'There was the most appalling scene because everyone got tangled up into the barbed wire and eventually someone had to be sent off to get wire cutters to release us all.' Brian's version was slightly different. He set the story in Warminster and had Hugh Burge, in mess kit, pinioned to the stage by the barbed wire while the audience laughed its head off.

His last few weeks in the Army seem to have been largely devoted to a round of farewell parties. Gradually the warriors dispersed; some returning to the jobs from which they had been so rudely interrupted; others seeking pastures new. In later years Brian, like so many war-time soldiers, seldom referred to these times and certainly never boasted about them. Nevertheless, friendships were forged which endured for years afterwards; the value of team spirit, something he had always approved, was confirmed even more; and the horrors and tragedies he witnessed made him even keener to devote his career to spreading happiness and light.

A good war, an odd war, brave and funny, admirable and enviable, and completely true to form.

8

All Demobbed and Nowhere to Go

Sound Bites Brian

At the end of the war Brian was thirty-three years old, entering middle age with uncertain prospects. Unmarried, unsure, he knew that the one career on which he had earlier embarked was not for him. There was no way in which he would return to that City office and sit behind his grandfather's desk sifting coffee grounds. Some men who had strayed into a war-time commission stayed on in the armed forces, but he knew that while he had made a decent if eccentric fist at war-time soldiering he could never have made a peace-time Grenadier. Not for him the desolate parade grounds of occupied Europe, exercises on Salisbury Plain, the endless dress rehearsal for a future conflict which might never happen.

When you left the forces at the end of the war you were issued with civilian clothes. Tradition had it that these suits were rather ill cut and ill fitting, so that 'the demob suit' became the subject of just the sort of music hall joke that Brian enjoyed – not that I have been able to find one in the Johnston canon. Brian however did have just such a suit, a blue pin-striped number which he collected from Olympia where they doled the things out. Then, thus kitted out, he went down to his mother's cottage near Aylesbury to consider his career.

Curiously enough, he doesn't seem to have thought of the BBC at first, even though it now, in retrospect, looks so obvious. After all, friends had been telling him he was a natural broadcaster at least since John Howard de Walden did so at Eton, around about the year – 1932 – when the fledgeling BBC came to rest at Broadcasting House, Portland Place, after beginning at Marconi House in the Strand and Savoy Hill.

It is easy to forget that broacasting only began when Brian was ten years old and at school at Temple Grove. That crystal and cat's whisker receiver that he remembered from those times must have been one of the very first. And by the standards of today broadcasting was, in every way, a curious not to say primitive affair. I can never quite believe that Lord Reith insisted that the BBC's radio announcers wore dinner jackets, but that is the legend. It is said also that in the early days would-be comedians were handed a card which said, 'No gags on Scotsmen, Welshmen, clergymen, drink or medical matters. Do not sneeze into the microphone.'

It would be interesting to know what Brian would have made of that.

In any event Brian seems not to have contemplated the BBC when he was first demobbed. He knew that coffee was out and he cut that umbilical cord by swiftly going round to the Brazilian warrant office and saying his farewells, expressing sorrow and contrition because he clearly sensed that he was, in a way, letting down the side and particularly the Johnston family interest.

Having done that he was quite lost. He would have loved to

be an actor, but he was too old to go to drama school or to negotiate some other bottom rung of the theatrical ladder. Instead he thought he might manage to find an opening on the management or production side. Various potential employers gave him interviews but they were uniformly dispiriting. It was hardly surprising. Former coffee merchant and Guards officer; amateur theatricals in Brazil and occupied Europe . . . these were hardly the sort of credentials to cut serious ice in Shaftesbury Avenue.

From a distance Brian sounds as cast down as he ever was in life. The ebullience and effervescence had all but deserted him. Then, as usually happened, something turned up.

'Something' was actually two 'somethings' in the form of the two famous BBC war correspondents with whom he had enjoyed such an enjoyable encounter during the war – the Canadian Stewart MacPherson and the Welshman Wynford Vaughan-Thomas. Brian was in the Guards Club, feeling glum behind a newspaper, when an old friend said that Stewart and Wynford were joining him for dinner and would Brian like to make up the four as he understood he was an old acquaintance. Brian agreed. A convivial evening ensued in the course of which Brian said he was looking for work in 'entertainment'. Next morning MacPherson phoned to say that there was a vacancy in BBC Outside Broadcasts and that the head of OBs would like to interview him. Brian must have been low because he admitted to being only 'mildly enthusiastic' and only agreed out of 'sense and good manners'.

When I spoke to Stewart MacPherson, then living in his native Winnipeg, he said he had had a feeling that night that Brian might turn out to be more trouble than he was worth. But he succumbed to Brian's charm and the two later became great friends. But I sensed a recollection of unease. 'Everything was a joke to Brian,' he remarked. I'm not sure if this is absolutely true but there were strong elements within the BBC which took themselves extremely seriously. They might not have appreciated a man to whom 'everything was a joke'. If Stewart MacPherson felt a twinge of apprehension at having introduced such a person you could hardly blame him.

The head of OBs was – perhaps inevitably in those days and given Brian's 'network' view of life – an Old Etonian. His name was Seymour de Lotbinière, otherwise known as 'Lobby'. Peter West, later to be a long-serving colleague of Brian's, described 'Lobby' as 'a man of lofty stature endowed with a most genial nature and a clear, incisive, cultured mind which analysed the content and delivery of a broadcast with the surest touch'.

Brian, less naturally deferential, wrote about 'Lobby' in terms, as usual, of anecdote. Before the war he had been staying with the Provost of Eton when Tubby Clayton, the famous founder of 'Toc H', was also a house guest. When Clayton was going to bed he was surprised to find de Lotbinière putting his shoes outside the bedroom door in the hope of getting them cleaned by morning. Ever the proselytiser, Clayton hailed him with 'What do you know about Toc H?' To which 'Lobby' retorted 'Nothing, thank God!' and shut the door. Within a short time, however, Clayton had converted him and used to boast, 'Lobby came to us as proud as Lucifer but we made him scrub floors.'

From which we can infer that S. J. de Lotbinière was a man with an open mind.

Brian was late for the interview. He said it was the secretary's fault. 'Lobby' seemed to forgive him and after questioning him for a while he said that Brian could try a couple of tests and if he passed them he would have a job. It might be temporary. It would certainly be badly paid. But it would be a job.

The first test was to go down to Piccadilly Circus and write a five-minute report on what he saw. Brian set off feeling at a loss, then noticed an advertisement in a shop window offering the chance to record your own birthday or Christmas greeting. Brian accordingly recorded his report on a disc, was appalled at hearing his own voice for the first time but succeeded in impressing 'Lobby' at least 'moderately'.

The second test was done with Wynford Vaughan-Thomas in Oxford Street. First Wynford conducted a series of live interviews. Then Brian followed suit. He asked passers-by rather obvious questions about rationing and somehow got through it. 'Ask a silly question,' said Brian, 'get a silly answer – always.' This became one of his favourite catch-phrases. Wynford seemed about as moderately impressed as 'Lobby'. At least Brian didn't dry. It would have been profoundly uncharacteristic if he had.

This recruitment procedure is certainly a long way from what happens nowadays, and one can't imagine John Birt condoning a system based on a chance encounter in the Guards' Club followed by a couple of five-minute vox pop mock outside broadcasts. But the times were different. Besides, perceived broadcasting skills were very different in those days. Today Brian would have been locked in a studio and fed interviewees by a producer and a squad of research-ers. In the late 1940s reporters went out on the street and reported. The autocue had yet to be invented. Talking to the man or woman in the street was a broadcasting art form. No one knew what a sound-bite was. It was all so very different.

Some days later 'Lobby's' secretary telephoned to say that

Brian had been accepted and was to report to Outside Broadcasts on 13 January 1946. He had embarked on the career that was to turn him into an institution as famous as and rather more loved than the BBC itself.

The bare bones of his professional life are easily summarised. 'Member of staff 1946–72. Cricket commentator 1946–70; cricket commentator TV 1946–70; cricket commentator on radio Test Match Specials 1970–; BBC cricket correspondent 1963–72; freelance: In Town Tonight, Down Your Way, ceremonial and royal occasions.' That was his own précis for Debrett's *People of Today*. His *Who's Who* entry was much the same.

Perhaps the first flesh to put on the bones was that in those days Brian was not keen on the BBC's image. In writing about this period he said that part of the reason that he had never given the BBC a thought was that he regarded the Corporation with 'a mixture of respect and tolerant amusement at its "Auntie" image'. Even some who were to become pillars of the BBC Establishment were exasperated by what they saw as its middle-class smugness. Richard Dimbleby, of all people, turned on the wireless while in the Western Desert with the Eighth Army after Christmas dinner in 1941 and simply couldn't stand it. He wrote later: 'The hearty voices of the announcers, particularly the patronising familiarity of the women, jarred and after half an hour we switched off.'

The Western Brothers even recorded a very Brian sort of song, devoted entirely to making fun of the Corporation and the sort of stuffed shirts who worked for it. It was called 'We're Frightfully BBC' and it began:

We're frightfully pukka, we represent town
Sent up to Magdalen and later sent down

Fellows of standing with people with crests
We've just had our colours tattooed on our chests
Rhubarb, tomato and rhubarb
We're really too utterly utter
As bored as two blighters could be . . .

And so on. The whole thing was delivered in a sort of languid
toffspeak with an air of infinite condescension. It was silly and
exaggerated but it contained some germs of truth. In some
ways, of course, Brian fitted the bill. He came from that sort of
background and education, but he hated people with airs and
he wasn't keen on lethargy and indolence.

So although he knew he was lucky to get the job he was
slightly ambivalent when he sat down at his first Monday
meeting alongside such stalwarts as his friends Stewart
'Shrimp' MacPherson and Wynford Vaughan-Thomas, Raymond Glendenning, Freddy Grisewood, Rex Alston, Audrey
Russell and even the famously irascible Gilbert Harding. The
very names evoke an era of steam radio which has long since
passed. These voices, so suggestive of tweed and pipe tobacco
(or in the case of Audrey Russell, twin-set and pearls), had
made their owners into household names. Television was still
in its flickering black and white, London and the south-east
only, infancy. The only rival to the wireless was the Press.
These people were stars. Today we would probably call them
mega-stars.

The OB department was divided into a number of different
sections and Brian, happily, was assigned to John Ellison who
ran 'entertainment'. This was right up his street, for one of
their main tasks was vetting West End shows to see if they
were suitable for live transmission. The usual form was to take
a half-hour extract which tended to rule out serious drama

and left 'Variety', musicals or farces. This was entirely to Brian's taste. Indeed for the first but by no means the last time in his life he was being paid to do what, left to his own devices, he would have done anyway.

For theatre managements these broadcasts were something of a two-edged sword. On the one hand they were good advertising but on the other they could induce a sense of *déjà vu*. Listeners who heard an extract on the wireless might be put off. On the whole, however, managements tended to be guided by the example of the Noel Gay show, *Me and My Girl*, which had been playing to half empty houses at the Victoria Palace until the BBC put it on air and business picked up to such an extent that it ran for another three and a half years. According to Brian the booking office was fielding phone calls even before the broadcast was finished.

Once Brian and John Ellison had persuaded management to let them make a broadcast, they selected appropriate passages and sometimes even altered the running order, occasionally with disastrous results. In one pantomime some Wicked Robbers were apparently done to death in Act One only to be mysteriously restored to life in Act Two. When it came to the actual broadcast Ellison or Brian would sit in a box and provide a linking commentary and explanation. This was entirely scripted and timed beforehand – there was no question of any ad-libbing – and it necessitated at least two or three visits to each show. In the case of his favourite, *Carousel*, there were evidently no fewer than fifteen. In the course of each one Brian admitted to being reduced to tears. (This particular show continued to have a remarkable effect on him for the whole of the rest of his life!)

Ivor Novello was a particular favourite, and Brian became friendly with the great man, even suggesting a different ending for one of his shows. The idea was apparently accepted.

Among the various musicals he saw in this way he always remembered in particular *Song of Norway* (his very first theatrical broadcast), *Oklahoma*, *South Pacific*, *Annie Get Your Gun* and *The King and I*, although for copyright reasons they never did *My Fair Lady*. His first 'theatre commentary' was a play called *Under the Counter*, starring the redoubtable Cicely Courtenidge and Jack Hulbert. In broadcasting terms the job called for 'perfect timing and crisp, clean delivery'. It was good training.

Even more fun for him was a weekly half-hour entitled *Round the Halls*. This was based on the same principle, except that the programmes came from all over the country and not just the West End. On the whole Brian's menu would consist of a singer or singers, a stand-up comic or cross-talking duo like Flanagan and Allen, and then a 'speciality act' such as an 'impersonator' or an 'instrumentalist'. On one notorious occasion in the thirties a broadcast from the Grand Theatre in Doncaster had bemusingly included jugglers and a paper-tearing act. However, by the time Brian joined the organisation it had become noticeably more professional.

A recurring problem was smut and innuendo. Max Miller was banned for his 'optician joke' – 'That's funny, every time I see F you see K'. Apart from sex there was a taboo on physical disabilities, the royal family, race, politics and religion as matters of humour. Denis Norden and Frank Muir, both of whom started writing for the BBC in the forties, apparently always wanted to begin a sketch with the line ' "Christ," said the Queen, "that one-legged nigger's a poof." '

By modern standards the rules seem impossibly prudish.

Brian used to claim that he was reprimanded for letting through an exchange which ran:

'Have you seen the PT instructress?'

'Oh yes, she's stripped for gym.'

'Lucky Jim.'

This has all the hallmarks of a vintage Johnston joke and remained in the canon for the rest of his life. Another old chestnut which seems to have got its first outing in this period was the one about the girl and the soap:

'I was walking along the beach here the other day and saw a girl bathing, and she was calling for help as she slowly drifted out to sea'

'Really. What did you do? Dive in and save her?'

'Nothing of the sort. I threw her a cake of soap.'

'Whatever for?'

'To wash her back, of course.'

That one was in Brian's posthumous book of jokes under 'X for crosstalk'. The words are slightly different but it's the same joke all right. Brian loved it and claims to have infiltrated it into an outdoor concert at Eastbourne.

Part of the fun, of course, was for comedians to sabotage the BBC by slipping in unscripted pieces of naughtiness. One such moment was when a supposedly drunk comedian took a swig from a glass of water from the table and spat it out with the words, 'I'll kill that ruddy cat!'

As Brian commented, the word 'ruddy' was acceptable though 'bloody' was not. Something of the same self-censorship permeated his own language. He never said 'bloody' and his only known swear word seems to have been 'Bugger!' which, in moments of particular excitement, he would repeat over and over again.

He was in his element with all this – 'slap in the middle of the entertainment world to which I had so badly wanted to belong'. The names of his new friends and colleagues are like a roll call from the early days of the Light Programme – Arthur Askey, Ted Ray, Tommy Trinder, 'Hutch', Terry-Thomas, Jimmy Edwards and, first encountered as 'unknowns' in a Jack Payne show in 1947 – Frankie Howerd and Max Bygraves.

However, even though it survived and looked quite healthy for a time, music hall was about to die. Television helped kill it, but radio played its part, for even as Brian and John Ellison were scouring the country for new material, so an increasing amount of light entertainment was being generated from within the BBC by a new generation of scriptwriters such as Norden and Muir. It was just as well that Brian was where he was and not trying to trip the light fantastic as a stand-up comic in the Alhambras and Empires of post-war England.

The atmosphere at Broadcasting House, or at least in Brian's part of it, sounds much like Mr Huson's house at Eton or the Grenadier officers' mess. Horseplay seems to have been endemic. There was no carpet on the floor of the large office he shared with John Ellison, so, naturally, they evolved a form of office cricket with a squash ball, a miniature bat and the waste paper basket. All bowling was under-arm, and you scored four for hitting the walls, six for the ceiling. You could be caught off ceiling or wall, and if you hit the 'in' or 'out' tray you were judged to have been caught. If you got the 'pending' tray it was LBW (Let the Blighters Wait). If the phone went during play, the caller was asked to wait until the end of the over. This even happened when Pauline's father came to see him. Colonel Tozer's view that Brian was 'a nut-case' was thus confirmed.

Years later, when Brian recorded *This Is Your Life* with

Eamonn Andrews, the game was recreated with some of the more famous players such as Denis Compton taking part. It looked rather stagey then, but at the time it was clearly boisterous fun.

In the same spirit the broadcasters were always telephoning each other using funny voices and false identities, to such an extent that none of them were quite sure whether any call was ever genuine. Brian's favourite hoax call was on his friend Geoffrey Peck. Peck took it upon himself to ask the famous 'Bouncing Basque', Jean Borotra, to be one of the match summarisers during the 1946 Wimbledon championship. However, when he mentioned this at the weekly meeting de Lotbinière did not seem as pleased as Peck had hoped. Evidently there was some question of Borotra having collaborated with the Germans during the war. 'Lobby' therefore told Peck to write to Borotra saying that there had been a change of mind but not offering a reason.

For Brian this was, of course, irresistible. As soon as he was back in his room he phoned Peck in a ludicrous *'Allo 'Allo* accent and told him with much Gallic enthusiasm how delighted he was to accept the BBC's kind offer. After a while an embarrassed Peck managed to explain that M. Borotra's services were not, after all, required. Brian immediately unleashed a torrent of *franglais* invective and told him that the Corporation would be hearing from his solicitors forthwith. He then put the phone down and went outside, where he was pleased to find an ashen-faced Peck going to 'Lobby' in order to warn him that they were to expect a writ from Borotra at any moment.

Brian, according to his account, let Peck tell his story and only interrupted when 'Lobby' reached for the phone in order to call the BBC lawyer. Then he put on his funny frog accent and the other two realised that they had been set up.

Most of his early broadcasts were rehearsed and scripted, although his very first was an eye-witness account of a bomb being detonated by the Royal Engineers in St James's Park. The bomb had been lying around in the lake since the war. Because it was his first broadcast Brian was accompanied by de Lotbinière himself. Originally they were to have watched from the bridge, but this was too dangerous so in fact he conducted the broadcast from a nearby ladies' lavatory where, by standing on one of the seats, he could just see out of the window. We only have Brian's word for this, and part of me is inclined to think that he invented it simply so that he could get a joke out of it. The joke, of course, was that he 'came out of that ladies' loo looking very flushed'.

There had been no mention of sport when he first joined, but there was a shortage of regular football commentators, so he, along with several others, did an audition at Queen's Park Rangers. Unfortunately QPR's star centre-forward was substituted shortly before kick-off without anyone letting Brian know. The star had scored a hat-trick on his previous outing and had been dubbed 'Three-Goal McGibbon'. Brian spent much of his commentary waxing lyrical about 'Three-Goal's' various idiosyncracies – only to discover, too late, that he had not been playing. Although he had been a fitful Arsenal supporter, soccer was not really Brian's game.

Then, out of the blue, he had a call from an old friend, Ian Orr-Ewing. Orr-Ewing was a Harrovian and had been at Trinity, Oxford, when Brian was at New College. During the Eton and Harrow match they used to sit in the same stand, now the Compton Stand, but then known more prosaically as 'Block G'. There was endless noisy barracking between the

Etonians and Harrovians, with Brian playing a conspicuous role. Several times the Eton and Harrow 'Block G' denizens played cricket against each other at the Hurlingham Club. For two years before the war Orr-Ewing had been on the staff of the fledgeling BBC Television. Now he was head of Outside Broadcasts and wanted to try televising some cricket from Lord's and the Oval. Would Brian like to do the commentary?

Cricket on television had hardly happened before then. On radio it was well established with E. W. Swanton, Rex Alston and John Arlott already installed, but at this stage only four Test matches had ever been televised – two in 1938 and two in 1939. The other television commentators in the first post-war years included Aidan Crawley (another Harrovian and a fine all-round games player), the former Surrey and England captain Percy Fender, and R. C. Robertson-Glasgow, who played for Somerset and vied with Neville Cardus for the title of the best cricket writer of the times.

As television commentators they were all beginners. Fender, in particular, seems to have got into frequent trouble for not holding the microphone close enough to his lips – his nose was as long as Brian's, which didn't help. 'Try holding it against your nose,' ordered an engineer one day. Fender turned to Brian testily. 'I am,' he said. But it was still too far from his lips. Brian had difficulty with the 'dirty talk-back' of the producer constantly coming through his headphones while he was giving his commentary. Not only do you have to acquire the ability to talk and listen simultaneously; you also have to avoid acknowledging the producer's instructions on air. Percy Fender was often crotchety when given instructions though he usually managed to keep his complaints to himself and Brian. My favourite story is of the producer who asked

'Crusoe' Robertson-Glasgow to give the score almost immediately after he had already given it. His 'on air' response was
to say, acidly, 'For those of you who were not paying attention
when I gave the score just now, may I repeat . . .'

'Crusoe', incidentally, was what Robertson-Glasgow was
habitually called but, for once, I don't think the nickname was
given him by Brian. As we've seen, Brian was already keen on
bestowing nicknames, some funnier than others. Some, like
'Floorboards', stemmed from some incident in the past; others
were word-plays: 'The Hatchet' for Neville Bury or 'Splendid
Chap' for Goodfellow. The least original were the ones that
simply involved putting 'ers' on the end of the first half of
someone's surname. Thus his own 'Johnners'.

No one seems able to pin-point the first appearance of this
sobriquet. 'Where did all this "Johnners" business come
from?' asked more than one old schoolfriend. John Woodcock, of *The Times*, who first met him at about this time, insists
that he was already known as 'Johnners'. Others seem less
certain.

His brother Christopher put forward a plausible theory on
the subject of nicknames. He thought there was more to it
than a delight in puns and *double entendres*. Brian, he reasoned,
was always eager to put people at their ease and liked to be as
matey as possible even if he had only just met someone. To
address a new friend or acquaintance by their christian name
would, in the world he came from, have been a dreadful
solecism. On the other hand, to use the simple surname would
have seemed too formal, even though 'correct'. The business
with nicknames was the obvious solution. It meant that one
could convey friendliness without being over-familiar.

True or not, the notion is persuasive. But even if, by now, a

101

few friends, such as 'Wooders', already knew him as 'Johnners', that was not how most people knew him. But at this stage, even though he was appearing regularly on the wireless and occasionally on television 'most people' did not know him. In 1948, however, he started to become seriously famous.

9

Let's Go

In Town Tonight

Much of today's radio still has a wonderfully ramshackle belt-and-braces atmosphere to it, but in the thirties and forties this was even more pronounced. The two top pictures on the back of the jacket of this book capture the times perfectly. The one on the left shows an eager Brian in suit, immaculate collar and tie, clutching a microphone of Heath Robinson style and proportions with the initials BBC prominently displayed on the top. The one on the right has Brian on a penny farthing bicycle with the sound engineer running along in his wake. A thick cable runs from Brian's waist to that of the sound man, looking for all the world like an umbilical cord. Primitive to a degree.

One of the Corporation's flagship programmes in the forties was *In Town Tonight*, produced by Peter Duncan. This was broadcast on the Home Service every Saturday evening and boasted some twenty million listeners. Television was a flickering small-screen presence, at first only available in London and the Home Counties, so a prime-time Saturday chat show on the wireless had a status unimaginable in these days of multiple choice cable and satellite TV. It was what people talked about in the pub at lunch-time on Sunday.

The introduction to *In Town Tonight* is therefore a masterpiece of self-confidence. 'This is the BBC Home Service,' says a Johnstonian voice and there follows a fanfare and a swish of military style music. Then you hear street noises, a newsvendor calling out 'In Town Tonight . . . In Town Tonight!' Then a voice calls 'Cut!' and in clipped, middle-class foxterrier tones the announcer says, 'Once again we stop the mighty roar of London's traffic and from the great crowds we bring you some of the interesting people who have come by land, sea and air, to be . . . IN TOWN TONIGHT.'

Most of it took place in a studio and was scripted and rehearsed to the last 'Good morning' and 'Goodbye'. Danny Kaye once caused consternation by picking up his script and throwing it all over the studio.

The only concession to spontaneity and the real world was a single regular outside interview spot. Originally this was Michael Standing's 'Standing on the Corner'. The title summed up the item. Standing stood on the corner of a street and accosted people, talking about anything that occurred to him. That the content was trivial and everyday seemed of little account. The fact that through the marvels of modern technology the BBC was able to interview a man in the street and broadcast it in twenty million homes around the land was sufficient in itself.

Gradually this miraculous novelty wore thin. 'Standing on the Corner' was replaced by 'Man in the Street,' in which Harold Warrender and Stewart MacPherson did much the same as Standing. Then Brian's boss John Ellison took over and changed the slot to something called 'On the Job'. This too was just what the title claimed. Ellison went to see people at their place of work and talked to them about what they did. Exciting it was not, but after a while Ellison was promoted to doing the scripted interviews in the studio and Brian took over 'On the Job'.

Even in his hands and on his own admission, 'Somehow it did not seem to amount to very much.' In the very beginning the novelty was such that a banal conversation sufficed, but after a while Peter Duncan realised that the outside broadcast slot was being wasted because it was simply duplicating what was already being done with greater ease and in more comfort back in the studio.

Before the war John Snagge had had a feature called 'Let's Go Somewhere', and Duncan and 'Lobby' decided to revive this with Brian in the Snagge role. The idea was to give him three and a half minutes of live, unscripted reporting which would involve something novel happening and might also contain that relative rarity in this sort of programme – jokes and a sense of humour.

This was grist to the Johnston mill. On 150 separate occasions over the next four years, and again later when 'Let's Go' was revived in the mid-fifties as a separate and much longer programme, Brian was able to tap his innate love of the jape, the stunt and the prank and carry it out for the delectation of the entire nation. It was as if he had been dressing up as that mad vicar at the Hirsel for public consumption and not just the amusement of the Douglas-Homes. Or pretending to be a starving beggar outside New College chapel for the benefit of millions. Indeed, on behalf of 'Let's Go Somewhere', he often dressed up and pretended to be a tramp or a lost foreigner talking an unknown and incomprehensible language. At their best these programmes were inspired and they made him famous years before he became identified with the game of cricket.

Brian has written about some of them and some tape recordings survive. Those who remember them will all have their favourites and the best do stick in the mind. John Wells, no mean impersonator himself in his role as Denis Thatcher, surprised me by being able to recite one of these broadcasts more or less off pat – and still laughing happily at the memory.

Their fun and humour is greatly enhanced, I think, by the fact that Brian's voice was appreciably higher pitched in those days and his delivery even more clipped and staccato than latterly. He definitely sounds a little like Harry Enfield doing the Mercury advertisements in pastiche 1940s style or the announcer on Pathe News.

This is how John Wells's favourite item began. There is no such thing as a typical 'Let's Go' broadcast, but these few moments perfectly capture the spirit of the show and its presenter at the time.

First the slightly pompous voice of John Ellison introduces the item from the studio in London.

There is a jaunty melody and then Ellison says, 'At about this time every year the Post Office asks the general public to co-operate with them by posting early for Christmas, so for "Let's Go Somewhere" tonight Brian Johnston has gone down to Oxford to see how the people there are helping to carry out this request. Well now, in order to get a grandstand view so to speak, without being seen he's hidden himself in a place in which I don't suppose any of you have ever been in your life. So let's go and join him now as he sits in this . . . rather . . . tight spot.'

A second later Brian's voice cuts in thus: 'Okay, well when I tell you that I'm extremely cramped and that I'm sitting in a

17. Brian joined the BBC's Outside
Broadcasts Department in January 1946.

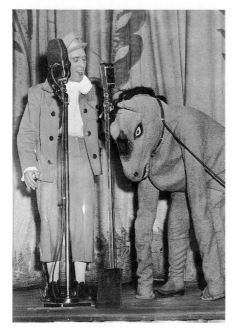

18. With Tommy Trinder.

19. Rehearsing 'the flying ballet'.

Let's Go Somewhere.

20. Excursion on the Flying Scotsman.

opposite
21. With Kenneth Horne.
22. As a GPO parcel.

23. Brian and Pauline were married at St Paul's, Knightsbridge, on 22 April 1948. Stewart MacPherson and Wynford Vaughan-Thomas were among those who made an archway of microphones.

24. Going to the BBC Riding Club fancy dress dance in 1950.

25. Brian and Bernard Braden commentate on the Coronation in Hyde Park, 2 June 1953, following the procession on a television monitor.

26. The early days of cricket on television, 1953; a lunch break with E.W. (Jim) Swanton at the Oval.

On holiday in
Polzeath, Cornwall,
June 1950.

27. The three
brothers, (*left to right*)
Christopher, Brian
and Michael.

28. Their three wives,
Charis, Pauline and
Barbara.

29. Pauline and Brian
with Barry, Clare,
baby Andrew and
Smokey the dog,
early 1960s.

30. Buckets of fun.

31. The cricketer.

space about two feet square and four feet nine high and that my voice sounds rather hollow and that every now and again something keeps hitting me on the head I assure you that I'm in a pillar box, a letter box . . . and I've got a load of letters at my feet here, I won't give the names away, but there are letters here addressed to Glasgow, Dublin, London . . . all the addresses very clearly written which is one of the things the Post Office . . . Aaah! that one hit me on the head . . . a package addressed to . . . Where's that going to? It's going to Reading.'

And so on. These broadcasts usually lasted three and a half minutes and this one concluded with Brian putting his hand through the slot of the box and personally taking delivery of a package from a very surprised member of the general public. In later years Brian used to say that she fainted but there is no evidence for this. However, one can say with some certainty that she was very considerably surprised.

Not all the 'Let's Go' ventures were as inventive and goonish as the Oxford post box episode, but the best have Brian's fingerprints all over them. My own personal favourite is the great Nottingham smash and grab raid, which belongs to the 'Let's Go' Mark Two series. This meant that it was much longer than the original episodes. Sometimes this could lead to slight *longueurs*, but not when, as in this case, he had a good situation and an inventive plot.

It was played to me by Ted Castle, who was the sound engineer on this enterprise. Like Brian's other sound men such as 'Spud' Moody, 'Nogs' Newman and 'Oggie' Lomas, Ted was fascinated by the technical challenge of these broadcasts and was an innovator of genius. It was he who, later, invented the now ubiquitous BBC 'radio car'. When I showed him a photograph of Brian wired up to a sound engineer with a thick cable, Ted sucked his teeth and said that he would never have done that. Somehow he would have contrived an invisible link, as he did the day on Victoria Station when he dressed up as a railway porter and had his box of tricks hidden on the trolley while Brian played the fool in the middle distance. That was the time he wore a wolf mask and a trilby hat to see if anyone took any notice. No one did!

The plan for the daylight robbery was simplicity itself. The only person completely in the know, other than the BBC, was the Chief Constable of Nottingham who had warned his men, in somewhat ambiguous terms, that 'an exercise' was going to take place. Nothing more specific than that.

'Brian was like a little kid,' said Castle, eyes glinting at the memory of the day. Their target was the jewellers in 25 Pelham Street, Nottingham. At the appointed hour Brian drove up to the shop, stopped, alighted, hurried to the window, smashed a pane of glass, snatched a handsome silver cup from the display, ran back to his vehicle, tossed his trophy on to the back seat, gunned the automobile into action and sped away just as the shopkeeper came scurrying out on to the pavement.

Throughout the smash and grab Brian keeps up a breathless commentary. You hear the smashing of the glass, the clunk as the cup lands in the back of the car, the slamming of doors, the revving of the engine and the changing of gears. As Brian makes his get away the broadcast cuts to police HQ where, dead on cue, Raymond Baxter is plugged in to the jeweller's SOS call. The jeweller has a strong foreign accent, is plainly agitated, but has managed to get a vague description of the vehicle and the letters on the number plate, 'LUW' – but not the figures.

Now the chase is on. Brian is speeding out of the city at

thirty . . . forty miles an hour, shooting red lights, peering in his mirror for signs of the constabulary. He spots a police car down a side road and acccelerates. Then another appears, closing in on him from behind. He knows he is doomed but he is not going to give up easily. When the police pull in front of him and stop, Brian mischievously starts up again. Over the air we hear a PC Plod voice saying, scratchily, 'He has ignored my signal to stop.'

At last the chase is over and a policeman approaches on foot. Rather cleverly he reaches through the open window and whips out the ignition key – an action approvingly described on air for the benefit of the millions listening at home. Then he goes through a wonderfully solemn routine of cautioning Brian, full of the familiar phrases such 'I have reason to believe' and 'Anything you say may be taken down and used in evidence . . .'

Brian has one last try at evading capture and as the policeman accuses him of being at 25 Pelham Street when the burglary took place, he blusters out the perfect Johnston alibi: 'Oh no,' he protests, 'it wasn't me. I've been at home playing bridge with my aunt.'

This is to no avail. The arresting officer says that Brian will have to accompany him to the station and Brian, magnanimously, announces to the nation: 'That is a completely fair cop.' He finishes the broadcast by extolling the virtues of the police in general and the Nottingham force in particular and then returns everyone to the studio.

Years later Ted Castle was passing through Nottingham and stopped off at the jewellers at 25 Pelham Street where he presented them with a copy of the tape recording. They were very pleased to have the souvenir, though it seems rather mean of the BBC not to have given them one at the time.

Oddly enough this episode is not part of Brian's own folk-lore. In writing or reminiscing about 'Let's Go' he seldom mentioned his burglary, and on at least one occasion misremembered and said it had happened in Brighton. Listening to it more than thirty years on, one is transported back to an age of charming naïvety as Brian canters through the charade with all the aplomb of Dick Barton Special Agent, facing up to PC49.

Brian's own selection of memories from 'Let's Go' ('I won't bore you with a complete list') begins at the very beginning with a night in the Chamber of Horrors, and ends with a balloon trip he made with Ted Castle from Cardington, in Bedfordshire, once home of the ill-fated airship R101.

I suspect he slightly exaggerates the horror of the Chamber, though despite the war-time gallantry he was someone who was often alarmed by threats which palled when compared to the guns of a German panzer division – spiders, for instance, or in this case the waxworks at Madame Tussaud's.

There was a rumour, in 1948, that Madame Tussaud's would pay £100 to anyone who was prepared to spend the night alone with the wax effigies of such famous real-life murderers as Doctor Crippen. Even the names and the descriptions of the villains have a dated feel – 'Smith of the brides in the bath . . . Mahon the Eastbourne trunk murderer' – and even though they were all dressed in their actual clothes and one of the props was the very bath in which Smith had murdered his brides, it is difficult to believe that a 36-year-old holder of the MC would be unduly disturbed by spending the night with them.

The rumour of the £100 reward turned out to be false. Nevertheless the head of publicity at Tussaud's, one Reg Edds, agreed that although no member of the public had ever been allowed into the Chamber after it closed at 7 p.m. an exception would be made for Brian and the BBC. Even so Brian wouldn't be allowed to stay after 11 p.m. when he would make the second of his two live broadcasts to the Home Service.

He made much of the experience – the frisson of fright when his head brushed the hangman's noose, the sudden juddering of massed mass murderers when a train on the Bakerloo line passed by underneath, the reverberations from the crunch as he bit into an apple supplied by Pauline, his newly-wed wife. It made an entertaining début for his new slot, if it lacked some of the wit and invention of the best of the later episodes. Pauline remembers him being white-faced with fright when he emerged.

His wife's apple is a reminder that his lucky break on *In Town Tonight* was not the only sea-change which made 1948 a water-shed year for Brian. Although in the past he had enjoyed close friendships with one or two ladies, he seemed in his thirties both to himself and his friends and colleagues to be a confirmed bachelor. He seemed happily set in his ways; he enjoyed a Boys' Own, clubbish, officers' mess sort of life; his job involved unconventional hours and frequent travel. He reminds one, in this period, of a latter-day Bertie Wooster, keen on japes, talking in an Oxford argot, with an eye for a pretty gel all right but no intention of getting hitched.

He always remembered the day Pauline phoned. It was 1 December 1947. Note that it was she who phoned him and not the other way round. Her brother Gordon Tozer, Brian's number two in the Grenadiers, had talked about him frequently to his younger sister. A couple of weeks earlier she had got a job in the BBC's photographic printing department, at The Langham. Gordon suggested that she should ring Brian up and tell him where she was working.

'But you might be wasting your time,' said Gordon enigmatically.

Two days after the initial phone call they lunched at the BBC club called the Bolivar, and the next day Brian invited her to go with him to the Chelsea Palace, where he was to broadcast a show with Dorothy Squires. When they met the star after the show, she asked perceptively, though prematurely, whether they were engaged. It was ten days after the first meeting that Brian did indeed propose. Pauline then 'played for time' but accepted on 5 January. Just a month had passed since the initial phone call. The Tozers, having got over the initial shock, wanted a June wedding, but that would have interfered with the cricket season, so Brian and Pauline were married at St Paul's Knightsbridge on 22 April. After the service, which was conducted by the Grenadiers' padre, his old friends and colleagues Stewart MacPherson, Wynford Vaughan-Thomas, Raymond Glendenning and John Ellison formed a guard of honour and made an arch of microphones rather than the more conventional ceremonial swords.

Inevitably, I fear, the honeymoon gave rise to two funny stories. The first was merely a coincidence. They shared the cost of the church flowers with another couple, the Tetleys, who were getting married the same day. The wedding night was spent at the Grand Hotel Eastbourne, where Brian's mother used to take him on 'going-out' weekends from Temple Grove. That morning at breakfast, who should be at the next table but . . . the Tetleys – looking equally exhausted, says Pauline waggishly.

The second half of the honeymoon was spent at Locarno in Switzerland where Brian developed a tiresome face-rash –

photographs of a bearded Brian survive and were shown amid much mirth years later during his appearance on *This is Your Life*. It was not so funny at the time because Brian had to have a course of injections which Pauline, luckily a Naval VAD, had to administer. They also had to buy penicillin, which used up much of their £25 foreign currency allowance. The only luxury they could afford was a single daily tea-time meringue at a lake-side café. The rest of the day was spent in their hotel room.

This was not an auspicious start, and when they returned home their temporary flat in Bayswater was small, bleak and largely unfurnished. Brian, whose father-in-law had failed to recognise him, shaved off his beard, and Pauline got on with the business of finding them a permananent home in St John's Wood as near as possible to his beloved Lord's. It sounds as if he was glad to return to business as usual. Indeed, Pauline recalls ruefully that against 22 April in his 1948 diary Brian wrote 'Wedding' – and ticked it off!

From time to time over his remaining years Brian allows a little of his family life to intrude into his public persona. Pauline's apple in the Chamber of Horrors is a case in point. By and large, however, he was a man who tended to live his life in quite separate compartments so that, for example, the friends of his youth did not as a rule get muddled up with his colleagues from the BBC. Brian, despite retaining many of the more obvious characteristics of the confirmed clubland bachelor, was henceforth a devoted family man. Not always a conventional husband and father, it is true, but from now on his wife, and later children, were always a precious part of his life. But because, on the whole, they were a separate, private part, I have given them their own separate chapter rather than try to weave them in and out of the fabric of his public career and personality.

Any involvement Pauline had with 'Let's Go Somewhere' tended to be as vicarious as the apple. On one occasion she actively objected to one of his adventures. This was when he took himself off to an East End tattoo artist's, and to Pauline's horror, had crossed cricket bats etched into his forearm. The tattoo mystified many who noticed it in later life – it seemed entirely out of character.

On another famous occasion Pauline watched from a distance as Brian did indeed 'halt the mighty roar of London's traffic'. The pretext for this performance was to find out whether or not people read the Personal Columns of newspapers. Brian had a friend who edited the now defunct *London Evening News*, and together they inserted an advertisement which read: 'Well set-up young gentleman with honourable intentions invites young ladies seeking adventure to meet him on the steps of the Criterion Restaurant, Lower Regent Street 7.15 p.m. Saturday, 19 May. Identified by red carnation and blue and white spotted scarf. Code word "How's your uncle?" '

Brian put the password in because he was pessimistic about there being a big enough response to justify a broadcast. Armed with 'How's your uncle?' he could at least call out to passers-by.

Pauline thought it would be fun to be in on this particular act but when, unknown to Brian, she arrived in Piccadilly it was clear that his lack of optimism was ill-founded. The place was packed; traffic solid, a cordon of policemen with linked arms holding back the crowd, hundreds of women and girls in all shapes and sizes and even some chaps with an eye to a main chance sporting red carnations and blue and white spotted scarves. It was chaos. Brian managed to fight his way into the Criterion, put on his flower and his scarf and stepped out on to the steps. No one apparently had realised that this was an *In Town Tonight* prank, but by now he was an instantly recognisable figure, so that when he appeared they realised immediately what was going on. There was a great chorus of 'How's your uncle?' He managed a few rather breathless interviews and then escorted two girls into the restaurant for a drink – together with their mothers, who had come as chaperones.

Next day the *People* had a front page splash revealing that a 'BBC Stunt' had started a 'Girl Stampede in Piccadilly'. On Monday a senior policeman telephoned de Lotbinière to complain. Unfortunately 'Lobby' was by now so used to Brian phoning him in a variety of silly voices that he assumed that the policeman was Brian. He was not going to be fooled this time and told the caller to get lost. When the policeman rang back 'Lobby' apparently realised his mistake and was able to explain all. One is reminded of Stewart MacPherson's prescient early thought that Brian might be 'more trouble than he was worth'. But as Brian himself recalled, 'I got away with it – just.'

Not all the episodes were as spectacular as this. His live description of giving blood was by no means as funny as the celebrated Tony Hancock spoof and was indeed more like propaganda for the Blood Transfusion Service. Some twenty or thirty of the broadcasts were akin to the 'On the Job' series, except that instead of merely interviewing people about the jobs they did, Brian actually had a shot at doing the job himself. At various times he was, as he recalled in *It's Been a Lot of Fun*, 'a cowman, RAC scout, wheel tapper, bell-ringer, town crier, ice-hockey goal-keeper, salesman on an exhibition stand, recruit in a drill squad and a toastmaster'.

However, many of the 'Let's Go Somewhere' antics were exercises in boyhood wish-fulfilment. In childhood he, like many of us, had read thrillers in which the hero had been trapped on a railway line and forced to lie prone between the rails as the express thundered overhead.

Brian decided to see if, in real life, this could be done and persuaded Southern Region to let him try on a section of track about a mile south of Victoria Station. In recounting the story he always emphasised that this was not as dangerous as it sounds, because there was a deep pit at this point in which it was possible to crouch in safety as the trains passed.

Nevertheless he was extremely alarmed by the whole exercise. The microphone lead had to be passed under live rails and Brian half expected to be electrocuted at any point. Remember that it was dark!

His original intention was to lie under the Golden Arrow as it set off for Paris, but the Golden Arrow was running late, so he had to make do with a common-or-garden suburban electric. Even so this was dramatic and alarming enough as it sped towards him in a halo of electric sparks. When it was thirty yards away Brian, commentating all the while, dived for cover and continued broadcasting as the train passed over him.

He was accompanied by a man from Southern Region, who told him that they couldn't move as the delayed Golden Arrow was now due at any moment on the same line. It was, as Brian always admitted, just as well that they were no longer on air. As the tardy express thundered overhead a passenger flushed the loo and Brian, in his own words, 'Got absolutely soused and my subsequent language would not have enhanced my BBC career had it gone out over the air.'

He, typically, makes a self-deprecating, funny story out of it. But at the time none of it can have seemed remotely funny.

Ted Castle also played me the tape of the other Victoria Station episode, when Brian persuaded the station announcer to make the following request over the Tannoy. It was cribbed from an old Richard Murdoch and Kenneth Horne show: 'I have a special announcement to make,' said Mrs Giles, the station announcer. 'Would passengers who took the 8 o'clock train from Platform 15 to Brighton kindly bring it back as we need it first thing in the morning. Thank you.' The first time she said this no one paid any attention. But the second time people did look up and laugh. 'That one really did get home,' commented Brian, chortling.

He rode a roller-coaster; he had cigarettes speared from his ears by a master dart thrower; on April Fool's Day he got Peter Sellers to impersonate him; he was shaved and shampooed on stage by the Crazy Gang; he rode bareback at Bertram Mills's Circus; was one of the Flying Ballet in the Ice Pantomime at the Empress Hall; sawed a woman in half; was sawn in half himself by Robert Harbin; played the back half of a donkey in *Puss in Boots* at the Palladium with Tommy Trinder; begged for money in the Strand; sang 'Underneath the Arches' with Bud Flanagan (thus realising a lifelong ambition); was attacked by a police guard dog (with Pauline playing the part of the lady with the handbag); and much else besides. Brian was game for almost anything.

After his first hundred and fifty performances he bowed out out on 17 May 1952 by being winched from the Solent by a Royal Naval helicopter, only to return with the second, longer and more ambitious series, some three years later.

Of all these programmes, however, his favourite seems to have been the one with which he celebrated his century. He toyed with various 'really sensational' ideas, but in the end decided to ask Peter Duncan if he could be seriously self-indulgent. His request was granted. On 24 February 1950 he and John Ellison appeared before a live audience with a compilation based on their shared experiences of music hall and variety. In it there are also obvious echoes of his own performances in Santos and with the Guards Armoured Division as well as a hint of what was to come with his much later one-man show in the 1990s. Brian liked to quote it in full, and in the interests of definitive documentation it seems only proper to do so again. Apart from being an exemplary essay in nostalgia it is also, incidentally, a plagiarist's delight.

It began with Ellison giving a 'serious monologue' called 'The Orphan's Return':

> 'Twas a dark cold night in December
> And the snow was falling fast,
> Little Nell lay in the gutter –
> And the snow was falling fast,
> Little Nell lay in the gutter –
> And the rich folk by her passed.
> You may ask me . . .'

Whereupon, enter Johnston with the words which he enjoyed uttering almost more than any other – 'I say, I say!'

JE. Yes, yes, what is it?

BJ. I've just seen forty men under one umbrella, and not one of them got wet.

JE. Forty men under one umbrella and not one of them got wet – it must have been a very large umbrella!

118

BJ.   Certainly not, it wasn't raining.

JE.   What d'you mean by coming on here and interrupting me while I'm reciting? Now go away. I'm sorry, ladies and gentlemen, I'll begin again – 'Twas a . . .

BJ.   It's in all the papers tonight.

JE.   What is?

BJ.   Fish and chips. We don't want London Bridge any longer.

JE.   Why not?

BJ.   It's long enough already. Do you know who's in the Navy?

JE.   No, who?

BJ.   Sailors. I've got a goat with no nose.

JE.   Really? How does it smell?

BJ.   Terrible.

JE.   I don't want to know about that. Will you go away?

BJ.   I've got a letter here. If I post it tonight, do you think it will get to Glasgow by Wednesday?

JE.   My dear fellow, of course it will.

BJ.   Well, I bet it won't.

JE.   How's that?

BJ.   It's addressed to Shoreditch.

JE.   It seems to me you're next door to a blithering idiot.

BJ.   Well, move over and give me a chance. By the way I nearly saw your brother the other day.

JE.   How do you mean, you 'nearly' saw my brother?

BJ.   Well, isn't your brother a policeman?

JE.   That's quite correct – he is a policeman.

BJ.   Isn't he PC 49?

JE.   That's quite right – he is PC 49.

BJ.   Well, I met PC 48.

JE.   You met PC 48 . . . Well, you may think you're very

clever, but let me tell you I've got a brother who even though he was on the dole, always managed to live above his income.

BJ. That's impossible, he couldn't be on the dole and live above his income.

JE. Oh! yes, he did. He had a flat over the Labour Exchange. By the way, what's *your* brother doing these days?

BJ. Nothing!

JE. Nothing? I thought he applied for that job as producer of *In Town Tonight?*

BJ. Yes, he got the job. They call him Button B, you know.

JE. Well, he's always pressed for money.

BJ. Well, I must say I don't know what your wife thinks about all this.

BJ. That reminds me, here's a letter from her.

JE. (*reading letter*). But there's nothing written on it.

BJ. No, we're not on speaking terms. Not that it matters, I've just got six months for rocking her to sleep.

JE. You can't get six months for rocking your wife to sleep.

BJ. Oh yes I can, you should have seen the size of the rock.

JE. I'm sick of this, let's go into this restaurant and get something to eat. Waiter, do you serve lobsters here?

BJ. Yes sir – sit down, we serve anybody.

JE. I see you've got frog's legs.

BJ. Yes, sir – it's the walking about that does it.

JE. How long will the spaghetti be?

BJ. I don't know, sir, we never measure it.

JE. I'll think I'll have some soup.

BJ. Right, sir – here it is.

JE. I say, waiter, there's a fly in my soup.

BJ. All right, sir, don't shout – all the others will want one.

JE.   Have you got any eggs?

BJ.   Yes, sir.

JE.   Are they fresh?

BJ.   Don't ask me, sir, I only lay the tables.

JE.   Oh! This is hopeless. I think I'll have a drink. What d'you suggest?

BJ.   I'd have a mother-in-law, sir.

JE.   Mother-in-law, what's that?

BJ.   Stout and bitter. Terrible weather, isn't it, sir?

JE.   Yes, terrible.

BJ.   I call it Madam Butterfly weather, sir.

BJ.   Yes, sir, ONE FINE DAY. But cheer up – just around the corner may be sunshine for you . . .

BJ *and* JE *sing together.*

Just around the corner may be sunshine for you,
Just around the corner skies above may be blue –
Even tho' it's dark and cloudy
Mister Sun will soon say 'Howdy'
Just around the corner from you –
We'll see you later,
Just around the corner from you.

'Well,' as the two of them would say, the English have been jesting like this at least since Antipholus and Dromio in Shakespeare's *The Comedy of Errors*, and the jokes haven't changed that much. Johnston and Ellison doing mothers-in-law and flies in the soup are not so very different from Antipholus and Dromio doing periwigs and excrement. On the page the jokes may look as 'old and corny' as Brian admitted they were, but taken in the right spirit and with 'real punch and speed' they can still work. That night in 1950 the

121

audience laughed and laughed and even – which apparently was unheard of on *In Town Tonight* – applauded at the end.

That he was allowed to get away with such a thing on the most popular wireless show of the week says something about Brian's standing in those days. As a jobbing broadcaster he turned his hand to anything, but it was *Let's Go Somewhere* which established him and made him as famous in the early fifties as he was to become, once more, in the eighties and nineties.

10

Master of Ceremonies

Speaking unto Nation

It's strange to hear Brian being solemn on old BBC tapes from the archives, and yet although his stock-in-trade was humour and a lightness of touch he was, like all BBC reporters of the times, expected to be a Jack of all trades. For years he and the ornithologist Henry Douglas-Home, brother of Alec and William, made ritual May-time recordings of nightingales in the grounds of Hever Castle. It's true that this gave rise to one of Brian's favourite funny stories when they stumbled on a courting couple in the bushes almost *in flagrante*, but they weren't intended to be humorous broadcasts. On these occasions Brian was meant at least to be serious if not actually romantic.

His first really sombre occasion was the funeral of King George VI. The BBC treated the King's death with such solemnity that for ten whole days they broadcast only on one channel with definitely no jokes. When it came to the funeral itself, with a naval gun carriage carrying the coffin through the streets of London followed by four royal Dukes and massive detachments of slow-marching servicemen, Brian's voice

123

metaphorically speaking, donned mourning and went into mellifluous Dimbleby mode. As, in the background, we hear the Dead March in *Saul*, his voice seems to have dropped several octaves and slowed to half pace so as to keep step with the procession he is describing. 'And . . . following the band of the Welsh Guards . . . comes the detachment . . . from the Royal Air Force . . . junior of the three services.'

The words don't exactly leap off the page, and it is true that Brian was never a poet of the airwaves in the fashion of several of his more lyrical peers. On the other hand he does manage *gravitas*, and it is noticeable that as the band performs its dirge-like task, he seems to be uttering barely two sentences a minute. Rare restraint for such a chatterbox.

Over the years he was frequently wheeled out for state occasions such as the Coronation in 1953 and the weddings of Princess Margaret, Princess Anne and the Prince of Wales. He was also on parade for the Queen's Jubilee in 1977. But he never became identified with this sort of broadcasting in the way that Richard Dimbleby did.

He also found himself a natural choice for commentating on the Sovereign's birthday parade, though, as he was the first to point out, drill was hardly a feature of his own service with the Grenadiers. His war-time service – most of his colleagues such as Dimbleby, MacPherson and Vaughan-Thomas, had been war correspondents rather than fighting soldiers – also meant that he was chosen to report the annual El Alamein reunion. This meant that every year he renewed contact with Monty. The two seem to have got on rather well, as is demonstrated by a noticeably friendly 72nd birthday interview Brian conducted with the Field Marshal on the 17 November 1959.

On the whole, however, he was happier operating in the

lighter vein which suited him best. The BBC certainly worked him hard. In 1962, for instance, quite apart from cricket and ceremonial, he was also appearing on *Sporting Chance*, (succeeded by a more general quiz show called *Treble Chance*), *Twenty Questions* and conducting the birthday interview on the old Jack de Manio *Today* programme – a much breezier programme in those days than the relatively abrasive modern version. He compered a new series called *Married to Fame* in which he chatted up the wives of the famous. On television he made one apparently uncomfortable forgettable appearance on *Come Dancing*, recorded in a huge ballroom in Purley, enjoyed an equally fleeting stint as a stand-in for Eamonn Andrews in *This is Your Life* (actually more of a 'warm-up' man than a stand-in) and joined David Dimbleby, Polly Elwes and Peter West in a television programme called *What's New*, which was a popular show about new inventions. It was rather less technical than *Tomorrow's World*, which succeeded it with Raymond Baxter at the helm, but the concept was similar.

A natural curiosity, particularly about trivia and ephemera, made him a natural for quiz shows and panel games. If he was able to indulge his passion for word-play then he was in his element. Just as 'Let's Go Somewhere' enabled him to play out his Boys' Own fantasies, so *Twenty Questions* and *Sporting Chance* meant that he could carry on doing over the air what he would otherwise have been doing with his friends and family. There was little respite, but on the other hand it wasn't really work in the accepted sense of the word.

'Busy B' was what Brian called this chapter of his life in *It's Been a Lot of Fun*, and there's no question about that. He was constantly on the go and, what with cricket and *Treble Chance*, often on the road. *Treble Chance* went to a different seaside town each week and he loved the English seaside, collecting and sending off ribald 'end-of-the-pier' or 'what-the-butler-saw' postcards wherever he went. His co-panellists were Nan Winton, Charles Gardner and his old friend Wynford Vaughan-Thomas, so it obviously *was* a lot fun. In fact it must have been rather like touring with a theatre company – just the sort of vaudevillian existence he had craved from childhood. His energy and enthusiasm were, as usual, boundless and he never complained. On the other hand, after the heady days of *In Town Tonight* his career seemed to have lost some of its momentum. He was an eminently respected and popular broadcaster, but far from being the national celebrity he had been and was to become once more.

In 1963 he was finally and crucially appointed the BBC's first official cricket correspondent. With the retirement of Rex Alston he was very much the BBC's senior staff cricket man. From now on his forays into general reporting became rarer and he became increasingly identified with cricket both on radio and television. However, that period in which he was to become almost the personification of the national summer game was yet to come to flower. And when that started to happen the omens were hardly propitious.

It was his son, Barry, who first drew my attention to the considerable fluctuations in Brian's popularity and fame. The sixties, such youthful optimistic years for so many, were really not a lot of fun for Brian. He was out of sympathy with the times, not least because Barry himself was a true child of the sixties. Visitors to the Johnstons' home during that period remember the positive embarrassment as Brian tried to carry on as normal while his teenage son was in his room smoking – some visitors wrongly assumed it was marijuana – strumming on his guitar or playing rock music on his record-player. Brian, ever the traditionalist, did not like it; was uneasy with the sudden overturning of old values and customs. He was particularly sad about the apparent contempt for authority which young people displayed, though, in fairness, he was never, as we shall see, in any way an authoritarian or disciplinarian when it came to his own children. He was far too easy-going and kindly.

In his public life the crunch came in the period between 1970 and 1972. It is easy to forget how old he was. Those apparently youthful pranks for *In Town Tonight* had actually been conducted by a mature gentleman approaching middle age. Born in 1912, he was, extraordinary though it may seem, over forty years old when the Queen was crowned, and the BBC had a mandatory retirement age of sixty. In 1972, therefore, he would be out on his ear with only a modest pension and few prospects. He was not, at that time, particularly well known any longer. It is quite significant, for instance, that when Mrs Callander, still the Johnston house-keeper today, first joined the family in 1960, she thought she might have heard of Brian but assumed he was the 'other' Brian Johnson (without the 't'), the singer whose greatest claim to fame was that he once won the Eurovision Song Contest.

The first blow was that in 1970 he was sacked from his post as cricket commentator on television. Although in public he always shrugged this off, it was a devastating upset which rankled for the rest of his life. He had done the job for twenty-four years, ever since being first signed up by Ian Orr-Ewing. He felt there was life in him yet and that he was doing a perfectly good job. The BBC didn't even have the grace to wait until his official departure two years subsequently. To make matters worse, he was never given an explanation; nor was he ever officially thanked for his contribution. To his close

127

friends and his family he confided that he felt not only saddened but humiliated as well.

I had hoped that the BBC might have some record of what happened. I asked Marmaduke Hussey, the Corporation's chairman and an old friend of Brian's – he also served with the Grenadiers during the war! – if there was anything in the files which might throw some light on the matter. Alas he told me that Brian's file only contained contract details and that no 'personal' file exists.

I also asked Peter Dimmock, who had been head of Television Outside Broadcasts at the time. He told me, 'There was really nothing at all sinister behind dropping Brian from the television commentary team. It was simply part of a carefully considered decision to begin to introduce ex-players to our sports commentary teams. An example of this was the introduction of Peter Alliss to take over from Henry Longhurst.'

In fact Jim Laker, the former Surrey and England spin bowler was brought in to the team which confirms this interpretation. It is slightly spoiled, however, because another of the casualties was Denis Compton, arguably an even greater cricketer than Jim Laker. Compton had been a regular in the television team since retiring from first-class cricket in the 1950s. Moreover Peter West, who had never played first-class cricket, was retained albeit in a new role as a presenter and interviewer.

Compton, who was as upset by his own sacking as Brian was by his, told me that he thinks it had something to do with politics, in particular South Africa. Both he and Brian were keen on South Africa, though they were adamant that this did not mean they were pro-apartheid. Peter Dimmock says this is nonsense and that 'I would have remembered had such an element been introduced when making our decision.'

Peter West himself thought both Denis and Brian 'the greatest fun' and was 'very sorry to see them depart the scene'. He believed, as everyone else did, that there was no explanation and no thank-you. He has described it as 'a woeful illustration of declining standards'. Brian never complained in public. In private he once remarked of the person, now I believe dead, whom he believed most culpable, 'That is a man I cannot bring myself to like.' This is almost the worst thing Brian was ever heard to say about anybody.

As it turned out, of course, the viewer's loss was the listener's gain. As Peter Dimmock says, 'In fact we did Brian quite a favour because not only did he build up an enormous following on radio, especially with the car commuters on their way home towards the closing stages of play each day, but also with the home radio audience, many of whom switched off the television commentary and watched the pictures with Brian's radio commentary! . . . The main reason was simply that his jokey style of commentary was, by then, far more suitable for radio than for television.'

This may be so, but at the time it did not seem like that. As far as Brian was concerned he was ignominiously sacked without an explanation or a word of thanks. Those who fired him did not, he felt, do so because they thought he could make a new career in radio. They simply wanted him off the screen. And, privately, he never forgot nor forgave. Indeed, although the BBC was such a huge part of his life, the Corporation was not always generous to him. His salary on retirement was only £10,000 a year.

Two years later he did retire from the staff of the BBC,

succeeded in his role as the Corporation's cricket correspondent by Christopher Martin-Jenkins, alias CMJ – a man more than thirty years his junior. Martin-Jenkins's association with Brian went back to his schooldays when, as an eager young Marlburian, he wrote to the great man to ask his advice on how to become a broadcaster.

It seemed like the end of an era. Brian packed up his office, and at one farewell party did a repeat of his cross-talk act with John Ellison, including one or two racy new jokes, such as:

'I must go now to see my wife.'

'What do you call her?'

'Radio 4.'

'Why on earth Radio 4?'

'Because she has nothing on after midnight.'

There was another farewell over drinks in the Governors' Dining Room and a dinner at Lord's from the Outside Broadcasts Department.

And then, like any good pensioner, Brian took himself down to the holiday home in Swanage to look back on his life and write his memoirs. 'The idea was,' he later wrote in his first volume of autobiography, 'that I should write this book there in peace, away from the telephone, and looking out to sea for inspiration. I have in fact written much of it there but have always found the sun and the sea more of a temptation than an inspiration, and have often found myself sneaking off to the beach.'

His had been a busy, interesting unorthodox life. Now he could hang up his microphone and enjoy his declining years in the bosom of his family.

11

Indian Summer

Country and Cricket

A retiring disposition was not a feature of Brian's character in any shape or form. Always one of nature's life-enhancing extroverts, he was also the possessor of an energy which made navel contemplation anathema to him. So the idea that, after finishing his career at the BBC, he would write his memoirs and potter about was never entirely realistic. On the other hand, the notion that he was about to embark on arguably the most successful period of his entire life was not one that anyone voiced at the time, nor was it one that even he entertained.

Brian always said he was lucky and that he got the breaks when they mattered. Now as a pensioner he was presented with two of the best.

As a jobbing reporter on staff he had always been a natural stand-in when someone else dropped out. He used to make a joke of it, remarking wryly but no doubt accurately, that as a staff man, he came free. Indeed on a BBC list of possible broadcasters there was a note against his name to the effect that in his case 'no fee' was required.

The exact date of his retirement as a staff man was 24 June 1972, but the preceding March an old colleague, Franklin, aka 'Jingle', Englemann, suddenly died of a heart attack. Englemann was one of those household names thought at the time to be completely irreplaceable. For almost twenty years he had been conducting *Down Your Way* on BBC radio, and had just completed his 733rd recording when he died. The programme itself had first started in 1946, when it was presented by the ubiquitous Stewart MacPherson and Richard Dimbleby. Englemann took over in 1953 and he and *Down Your Way* had become virtually synonymous. He had one of those comfortable middle-class tweed and pint of bitter voices which were so much of that period in the BBC's history. The programme itself was perfectly suited to this style for it represented the ultimate in cosy, reassuring British Broadcasting conducted to a formula of utter simplicity.

In a way it was really just an extended version of the old 'On the Job' interviews which Brian had done for *In Town Tonight*. The essence was wonderfully simple. Basically you chose a town or village, more or less at random, then gleaned half a dozen names from the phone book, knocked on their doors, had a genial chat and asked them to select their favourite piece of music. Not exactly challenging.

The sub-text to Brian's original assignment is fascinating. Englemann died on the Wednesday night, hours after recording the show. It was due to be broadcast on Sunday and there was nothing in the can for the following week. Unless the series was to be aborted, a new presenter had to be found to go to Hyde in Cheshire to do the next programme. Thus – as if fate had decreed it – the ever willing Brian was asked to step into the breach.

Not that he was an automatic choice for the job. His story

was that he was walking down the corridor at Broadcasting House on the Thursday after Englemann's death when a door opened and out popped Arthur Phillips, the producer. Phillips asked if he had heard 'the sad news about Jingle'; Brian said 'no', whereupon Phillips told him and, almost in the same breath, asked if Brian could fill in for the dead man the following week.

The Hyde experience must have been a slightly spooky one, and Brian was careful to conduct himself in a reverential manner beginning with an apology for 'intruding'.

However, it passed off satisfactorily enough. Brian had a soft spot for Cheshire ever since the Eton Ramblers' August cricket tours of the 1930s, when they had gone to Blackpool to gawp at the Rector of Stiffkey and the substantial 'Buns' Cartwright had got on to 'speak your weight machine' and been admonished, 'One at a time please!' Mind you, Brian's Eton Rambler Cheshire was some way removed from the Greater Manchester of Hyde. His idea of the county was typical of his idea of England: 'Black and white magpie houses, lots of woods and meres and cattle grazing in lush green meadows.' This was England, his England, and it was partly because he had this romantic vision of his homeland that he suited *Down Your Way* so well.

He then went on to make another ten programmes before leaving for his last full summer as the BBC cricket correspondent – although his retirement was technically in June, it had been decided that he should stay till the end of the season and formally retire on 30 September.

Four other broadcasters filled in on *Down Your Way* during this interval, but none superseded him, and in the autumn, now freelance, Brian returned to fill the slot which was to help make him one of the nation's best-loved figures.

During his fifteen years on *Down Your Way* he sauntered off from St John's Wood just before Wednesday lunch-time every week and came home the following evening or, depending on the length of the journey and the recording schedule, late on Friday. For the final two years the programme, in common with all other Radio 4 regulars, took an annual six-week holiday, but until then *Down Your Way* actually went out at five past five every Sunday afternoon throughout the year. In order to be able to take a holiday themselves, the *DYW* team sometimes had to double up and record two programmes in a single week. Sometimes Brian seemed to be forever on the road. And remember, this was a retirement job. When he finally drew stumps on himself he was only a month short of his seventy-fifth birthday.

It was always a team job, though the nature of the beast was that it was perceived to be very much an extension of Brian himself – just as it had been of Franklin Englemann in his day. For most of the programme's run the producer was the BBC's Anthony Smith, and it was he who chose the locations and selected the interviewees. He would be on site well before Brian's arrival, to prepare the ground.

Originally – and this is typical of the belt and braces broadcasting of the early days – there was virtually no preparation. Stewart MacPherson's producer, John Shuter, apparently used to pick part of London and select names at random from the phone book. On the appointed day MacPherson simply went round knocking on doors unannounced. They only abandoned this happy-go-lucky approach, according to Brian, when an irate husband opened the door and accused MacPherson of being the man who was pursuing his wife. Too good a story not to be in Brian's repertoire even if apocryphal.

In Brian's time the drill was that he would rendez-vous with Smith over dinner at their hotel on Wednesday evening. Business was never discussed until social pleasantries had been exchanged. There would be talk of cricket, of family and friends and then, Brian being someone who liked traditional unchanging catch-phrases in much the same way that he loved old jokes and *Hymns Ancient and Modern*, would always produce the identical question, 'What have we got tomorrow, Old Boy?'

Smith would then run through the following day's schedule and Brian would then retire for his usual early night. Next day, after breakfast – he preferred to take this meal undisturbed – Brian would be ready and eager for the off, bags packed, bill paid. 'Then for six hours without stopping,' Smith recorded in his tribute to Brian, 'we would go from cottage to castle, from farm to factory, recording our interviews.'

His partnership with Smith was obviously warm and effective, commemorated by Brian with a valedictory silver tankard inscribed with a handwritten message thanking Smith for 'so many happy days of fun and friendship'. Before Smith, however, his producer, albeit comparatively briefly, was a woman, Carole Stone. She remembers, with a certain wry amusement, how awkward Brian could sometimes seem when, as often happened, the two of them had to dine alone. He always, she recalled, began with a glass of sherry, was politeness itself throughout the meal but 'rather embarrassed . . . and uncomfortable'. Always, at nine thirty sharp, he would say, 'I must go and ring Pauline', and shuffle off – rather relieved, she felt – to bed.

Down Your Way was bland stuff. Even Brian was fond of saying that 'it may all sound rather square', but that was the way he wanted it and consistent listening figures of about a million bear witness to his acumen. He was putting into practice the Prince Charles / Martyn Lewis theory that there *is* such a thing as good news and that people like to hear it. 'When we visit a place,' he said, in the programme's heyday, 'we never look under the carpet for any controversy or scandal. We go for the good things and nice people and it is gratifying to find so many of both in our so called sick society.'

Everyone agrees that there was never any artifice or contrivance in this. He was simply doing what came naturally and, by being friendly and relaxed and positive, he managed to encourage other people to be the same. Each of his interviewees was allotted an hour. The first twenty minutes would be an off-air warm-up, during which Brian would occasionally scribble a note on a reporter's pad – generally just a single word prompt. Then when he was ready he would pronounce a single well-worn phrase, 'Well, I'm broody.' Actually Brian's own version was slightly different. He said that his actual words were, 'Well, I'm feeling broody now. What about us recording our conversation?' He was particular about this because the word 'conversation' was important. He avoided the word 'interview' because he didn't want to seem like an interrogator. Instead he wished to come across as a chum. Nevertheless both Smith and Johnston are agreed that the word 'broody' always came into it. A curious word, though an agreeable concept: the broadcaster as hen, laying what he hoped would be golden eggs. It was rather like saying grace. 'Broody' meant he was ready to begin.

For fifteen years he soldiered on until 20 May 1987, when he equalled 'Jingle's' record of 733 shows and decided that it would be unsporting to surpass him. He bowed out with a valedictory *Down Your Way* at Lord's Cricket Ground, where the scoreboard duly recorded 733 against the words 'Last Man'. It was the highest score ever registered underneath the famous Old Father Time weathervane. He posed for a commemorative photograph in front of it, toothy-grinned in a light grey pin-stripe, with a polka-dot handkerchief peeping from the breast pocket, a vivid rhubarb and custard MCC tie at his neck, and a Gray-Nicholls cricket bat held aloft with the inscription *'Down Your Way*. Brian Johnston. 733 not out.'

He said it made his day, and the gilt on the gingerbread was that the final interview was with his friend and former TV colleague, Denis Compton, whose association with Lord's was even more intimate than Brian's. Denis's choice of music was 'My Way' sung by Frank Sinatra. 'All in all it didn't seem out of place to play me into the Pavilion, so to speak,' wrote Brian. It was his sort of tune and his sort of sentiment.

Over the years he reckoned he had interviewed about 4,500 people on *Down Your Way*, and he travelled all over Britain as well as to Australia to do it. Former interviewees often wrote to him or would greet him in the street or at cricket matches just as if he were a long-lost friend. This he encouraged and it was just that spontaneous offering of friendship which permeated the programme and made it such a good deed in a naughty world. As Tony Smith puts it, 'Brian's approach to life and his warmth and personality evoked this kind of response.'

This is true, but one must never lose sight of the professionalism either. For example, each of his conversation companions got an hour. This included warm-up, recording and a de-brief, which might just consist of a drink or slice of cake (as on *Test Match Special*, cake became an occupational hazard), or could involve a tour of the work-place. The only exception was for the very old who sometimes rambled. One would normally expect this routine to be strictly governed by reference to the clock, but Brian always claimed that throughout the exercise neither he nor Tony Smith ever once consulted their watches. Brian, typically, used to shrug this off with a self-deprecating line about 'getting it off pat'. But actually it involves professionalism of a high order.

Brian himself was, I think, anxious to appear amateur without actually being so. Others disagree about it, and perhaps in the end it is just a question of semantics. John Woodcock, for instance, told me that he never thought of Brian as a professional but as the very best sort of amateur. By this he didn't mean that he was slack or haphazard. It was more a question of attitude. My own view is that Brian liked to appear effortless and casual but only did so as the result of considerable homework. The friendliness which, above all, was his distinctive hallmark – never more so than on *Down Your Way* – appeared as effortless as the timekeeping, the background knowledge and the verbal felicity. I can't help feeling, however, that there must have been occasions when he would have needed to work hard at that too.

It was this quality of friendliness as much as anything which endeared Brian to the army of fans who so loved him on *Test Match Special*. Brian always claimed that much of his success was down to fluke or happenstance: being in the right place at the right time, bumping in to Stewart and Wynford when he did, walking down that particular corridor just after poor old 'Jingle' Englemann dropped so unexpectedly dead.

In the case of *Test Match Special*, however, he was righter than usual, for although the programme became a personal triumph that was not how it started out. The sacking from television cricket was, as we have seen, ignominious, and he was now a sixty-year-old pensioner. Besides which he was out of kilter with the times and particularly with the new atmosphere at the BBC.

Tim Matthews, who worked with Jack de Manio on the *Today* programme, remembers Brian standing in as de Manio's substitute – yet another stand-in role! Matthews, who served with the Irish Guards, enjoyed Brian hugely. 'He was one of those people who always made you feel better the moment you saw him,' he says. 'He had something in common with Wynford and Jack. They were eternal school-boys. Also they had an innate dislike of bureaucrats and organisers.'

Matthews says that there was a sharp division within the Corporation between 'gents and non-gents'. The non-gents tended to be bureaucratically inclined, orthodox and rather humourless. Bringing in the serious, flat-vowelled Yorkshire-man Jim Laker on television in place of plummy, facetious Brian was an obvious manifestation of this. It wasn't just a class distinction, it was just as much a difference of style.

'Jack and I,' remembers Matthews, 'were accused of appealing to the drunk widows of retired air commodores in the Cotswolds.' This was a calumny but it contained an element of truth. The programme, in the de Manio days, always contained a sense of barely suppressed – sometimes completely unsuppressed – chortle which was very Brian. One small story encapsulates this approach. In those days there were two separate editions of the *Today* programme and in the interval between them the team had breakfast together. Brian was appalled by the sogginess of the toast and complained loudly and persistently. Eventually a toast rack was provided, known for the rest of its life as 'the Brian Johnston memorial toast rack'.

There is a very real sense in which broadcasters then were divided into those who cared about toast and toast racks and those who didn't.

Until Brian joined, the broadcasting of Test match cricket was conducted along rigorously un-'toast rack' lines. Commentators and summarisers were expected to report and analyse the game in a serious, no-messing-about manner. There were definitely no jokes. Indeed Robert Hudson, head of Radio Outside Broadcasts, had written a memorandum about the style required of the cricket commentators which included stern stipulations about jokes, undesirability of.

In the early seventies this changed. The advent of Brian, least strait-laced of broadcasters, undoubtedly had something to do with it, though BBC folklore has it that it was the advent of Cliff Morgan, first as head of Sport Radio and then in 1974 as head of Radio Outside Broadcasts, which produced the vital change. Morgan, a noticeably natural and conversational broadcaster, as anyone who listens to his Saturday *Sport on Four* will know, felt that the Corporation's cricket coverage was too starchy.

It was also customary, when rain stopped play, for listeners to be 'returned to the studio' while improving music or talk would be transmitted until the cricket resumed. When this happened the commentary team would chat among themselves. Some of them, including Brian, felt that these conversations were so entertaining that the public should be allowed to eavesdrop on them. This was agreed and a tradition was born. Purists did not always approve – even participating purists such as John Arlott. 'Immense interest,' he once wrote, grumpily, 'obviously has been generated by the casual chat which goes on when rain stops play and is often

– in this writer's opinion, unpardonably – quite unconnected with cricket and irrelevant to the situation.'

This view enjoyed some support and there was even an outbreak of strong hostility in *Wisden Cricket Monthly*, but by and large the punters loved it. As Arlott recognised, though I sense he deplored it, 'It has appealed to many listeners relatively unconcerned with the course of play.'

Brian's starting point, which would not have found favour with true cricket zealots, was that the game '*can* be dull'. Bearing that in mind, he wrote: 'Our approach is quite simple. Five or six of us go to a Test match for just the same reasons as other spectators – except that we luckily don't have to pay! We go to have fun and enjoy ourselves, and even have the odd glass of something. Our aim is to behave naturally as a party of friends would. Never miss a ball but if one of us has received an interesting letter or been told a funny story then we share it with the listeners. The word *naturally* is important. It means – to be ourselves in front of the microphone.'

This comes as close as anything to capturing the essence of *Test Match Special*'s appeal. Its single most vital characteristic for the general listener was the sound of Brian having a day out with some chums. Several writers have tried to explain this but, at the end of the day, the secret magic is elusive because it is ephemeral and of the moment. When Brian broadcast from a Test match he did not have an eye on posterity; he spoke, like any good broadcaster or journalist, with only his immediate audience in mind. For this reason the word-by-word transcript seldom stands the test of time and subsequent generations will find it hard if not impossible to understand what the fuss was all about.

John Arlott, not always temperamentally in tune with Brian, was revealing about his most characteristic trait.

Paying tribute to Brian's ability to defuse argument, rivalry or other unpleasantness in those cramped, competitive commentary boxes, he wrote that there was so much leg-pulling that pomposity was impossible.

One of the hardy-annual practical jokes – invariably perpetrated by Brian Johnston – is to hail a commentator coming into the box when it is off the air by saying into the microphone, 'Ah, here is so-and-so, and I know he will have strong views about this. Tell me, so-and-so, what do you feel about such and such?' Simultaneously he moves out of his seat and waves the newcomer into it. The joke lasts as long as the other occupants of the box can refrain from bursting into laughter. The joke is possible only because of the essential difference between sound radio and television commentary points. Television commentators work on lip-mikes which only gather sound when held close to the mouth. There they have too a 'lazy' mike through which they can talk to the producer without the listeners hearing. Sound radio, though, employs sensitive 'open' microphones which pick up virtually anything said within six or eight feet. For that reason anyone who does not know whether the mike is alive or not is in a quandary: he cannot ask the relevant question. More than one man – including the writer more than once – has been caught out through assuming that Johnston is pulling his leg when actually the microphone is live. Then the result is staggeringly embarrassing.

Another Johnston stock-in-trade was to wait until a colleague had just popped an outsize piece of chocolate cake into his mouth and then pose a particularly difficult question. Nothing he liked more than seeing someone trying to talk to the nation with a mouthful of cake!

I infiltrated the *TMS* commentary box for the first and only time at Leeds in the summer of 1989. I seem to have been rather disrespectful about Brian, describing him, in the *Daily Telegraph*, as 'an avuncular old cove in a canary yellow pullover and perforated brown and white shoes of a sort not often seen outside the Drones Club'.

I was lucky enough to be present during a small episode which neatly summed up the essence of the programme's popular appeal. Brian was beaming away at the Australian, Steve Waugh's batsmanship when the door of the commentary box burst open and there was a uniformed policewoman holding a cardboard box. Behind her there was a policeman in a helmet who pointed at Brian whereupon his colleague advanted on our hero and gave it to him, rather, as I wrote at the time, 'as if presenting a summons or parking ticket'. You have probably guessed by now. It was a cake, complete with iced cricketers on top – a gift to Brian from the Traffic Division of the Leeds Constabulary.

During the tea break Brian, at the microphone, thanked the police, identified PC Pearson, now out in the middle, guarding the wicket, said he was now free to drive at 70 m.p.h. through the city centre, and turned to the gnarled old pro on his right.

'You ever been given anything by the Leeds police, Fred?' he asked.

At which 'Sir Frederick' Trueman, the old Yorkshire and

England fast bowler, removed the pipe from his teeth and growled, 'Only a speeding ticket.'

Johnston, the jolly southern card, Trueman, the grumpy northern rough diamond, both knew their parts and stuck to them. Part of the charm was that you always knew how they were going to behave and very nearly what they were going to say. One BBC mandarin is supposed to have complained that since they were so predictable in everything else, why couldn't they let the Corporation know exactly when the next wicket was going to fall. Enough said.

Brian didn't speak like anyone else on radio. Like other great broadcasters he had a unique voice and a unique dialect, known, I am informed by *The Times*'s word expert, Philip Howard, as an 'idiolect'.

Howard, discussing Brian's use of English, explained that 'Every articulate and literate human being has a particular way with language which is distinct from all users and abusers of that language.'

In Brian's case Howard focused first on his delight in 'bad puns, innuendoes about private parts and silly malapropisms'. The most famous of these, of course, was the Botham 'leg-over' incident, of which more later. But others passed into *TMS* lore. 'The bowler's Holding, the batsman's Willey' was arguably the most inspired. Other famous, possibly less contrived favourites, were the 1961 observation of Neil Harvey, that he was 'standing at leg slip with his legs wide apart waiting for a tickle' and another in 1969 when the New Zealander, Glenn Turner, was hit, painfully, in the box. Brian's comment when the batsman carried on was, 'Very plucky of him. Yes, definitely going to have a try. One ball left.'

When Peter Pollock, the South African, twisted an ankle,

Brian commented, 'He's obviously in great pain. It's especially bad luck as he is here on his honeymoon with his pretty young wife. Still, he'll probably be all right tomorrow if he sticks it up tonight.'

Connoisseurs of the Johnston idiolect will catch echoes of the joke from the wartime Guards Division review about the honeymoon couple on the bicycle made for two.

Not everyone was amused. His colleague, Alan Ross, sometime cricket correspondent of the *Observer* and editor of the *London Magazine*, told me that he couldn't be doing with this kind of prep school smut. However he remembered one occasion, on a foreign tour, when he found himself dining alone with Brian. For once, recalled, Ross, the flippancy was cast aside and the two enjoyed a long and interesting conversation about the problems of after-dinner speaking. Ross was surprised – and impressed. However, most people loved the schoolboy humour and Brian responded accordingly.

The other characteristic Johnstonism identified by Philip Howard was the 'Johnners' syndrome, his habit of abbreviating words and adding the suffix 'ers'. Howard says this came from Oxford in the 1930s and he cites such examples as 'memuggers' for memorial and 'wagger-pagger-bagger' for waste paper basket. Apparently the usage originated at Rugby School in 1875 and later spread to the Armed Services, who prefixed the form with the word 'Harry'. Thus 'Harry screechers' meaning drunk.

Brian would have been amused by this scholarship but not much bothered. The point in the end was, as Howard observed, that 'No student at Oxford or any other university has used such daft slang for fifty years. It is obsolete and absurd. The jokes were puerile and rude. But because he loved what he was doing Johnners changed the language and sent it up. This would have made him giggle, but he had more influence on the native tongue than most professors of English.'

It *would* have made him giggle, but it would have pleased him too. And it is probably true.

For more than two decades Brian was the keynote figure in what was as much of a running soap opera as his latterday favourite *Neighbours*. The cricket itself was crucial but, almost, incidental. The rest of the cast, all suitably nicknamed – 'the Alderman', 'Blowers', 'the Boil', 'Sir Frederick', 'the Bearded Wonder' – were all imbued with particular characteristics and then happily played up to them. As old stalwarts like Rex Alston and John Arlott were written out of the script, so new ones like 'Aggers' or the Australian 'Dr No' arrived to take their place.

When you read the transcripts you indeed wonder more often than not – even in the 'View from the Boundary' interview slots which filled much of the Saturday lunch interval – what made *TMS* such a cult success. The answer is that to appreciate fully the significance of Brian's perform-ance you needed to be there listening live on a fine June day, perhaps sitting in the garden with a glass of Pimms and a smoked salmon sandwich, not mowing the lawn but drinking in those timeless, mellifluous cadences wafting out of the radio and into the ether, casting a spell which made little boys out of everyone and gave us cause to be pleased, for once, to be English and alive, even if we were being thrashed by the old enemy from down under.

It was magic.

12

The Love of Friends

The Alderman, Wooders and Others

In 1976 the whole of the Saturday of the Lord's Test against the West Indies was rained off. Undaunted, Brian and the team talked on. It was a broadcasting *tour de force*.

The following Monday Brian arrived in the commentary box looking extremely pleased with himself. His friends at Buckingham Palace, he told his colleagues, reported that Prince Philip thought the *Test Match Special* boys had acquitted themselves particularly well. Brian, apparently, was inordinately pleased by such a shameless name-drop.

I was puzzled at first when I read this story because for all his connections I didn't really think of Brian as someone who was constantly in and out of the Palace. Of course he would have been there in 1983 and 1991 to receive his OBE and CBE from Her Majesty. Then I remembered that I had sat next to a distinguished person at Brian's memorial service in Westminster Abbey. The friend in such a high place was probably his old school chum 'Ned', aka Sir Edward Ford, sometime Assistant Private Secretary to the Queen and a St John's Wood neighbour. In fact Pauline says it was his old colleague John Haslam, who had moved from the BBC to the Palace press office.

Brian did not just have friends in high places; he had them in most places. Moreover, although obviously blessed with a network of rich, aristocratic and powerful chums, he was careful not to pull rank or act snobbishly. At least one BBC colleague found him almost defensive about his service with the Grenadiers. He was tremendously proud of it, but he preferred not to draw attention to it in front of people who might have an attitude problem about the Brigade. In the same way he made a point, at regimental dinners, of not being placed at a top table or even among his brother officers. He preferred to sit with the men.

Friends help to define many people, but Brian more than most. He had a natural capacity for friendship, but he also appreciated that friendship which looked natural and easy was something that had to be worked at.

And he did. More than one of his old schoolfriends told me that Brian was the one person who could be relied on to know what everyone else was doing and how they were. 'I wonder what happened to old Carruthers?' chaps would ask. 'Planting tea in Assam,' Brian would reply, quick as a flash, or 'farming sheep near Waikato'. Pauline remembers him disappearing to his study upstairs and working his way through his phone book, methodically checking up to make sure that his friends were all in working order.

It would be invidious to single out particular friends. Brian would not have wanted that. Nor, as far as I can see, did he ever do it during his lifetime. As his great friend, William Douglas-Home, once wrote, 'I have been lucky in my friends over the years ... This does not mean that I have special favourites. I delight in all of them, regardless of their origins or the impact they may – or may not – have made on life.'

These are very much Brian's sentiments, though there doesn't seem to be much doubt that Douglas-Home was a very special friend, not least because they went back such a long way and had shared so much from schooldays onwards. Of Brian, Douglas-Home said, 'He was very friendly, always laughing, always helpful, totally unpatronising and a good companion, much admired by boys and masters alike.'

This appears to be the universal verdict of those who knew him at school and who so often remained friends until, literally, death did them part. Douglas-Home predeceased Brian, and it seems that Brian was profoundly shocked and upset by his death. Characteristically, says Pauline, he never ever referred to it. It was too upsetting to be mentioned.

More than one of his most longstanding friends asked me about his nickname in terms of some incredulity. 'Where did this ridiculous "Johnners" business come from?' Lord Howard de Walden wanted to know. This happened so often that I invented a rule of thumb: that anyone who referred to him as 'Johnners' came from a post-war vintage of friends. Certainly I feel that friends like William Douglas-Home, Jimmy Lane Fox and John Hogg belonged in a different category to those – even men like Wynford Vaughan-Thomas or John Woodcock – who came later into his life and hadn't shared the same seminal experiences. It is not that they were 'better' friends. Brian would have been horrified at the suggestion. But they were different.

Of course to the world at large during the last years of his life Brian's friends were the friends they heard him joking along with on the wireless, the stalwarts of *Test Match Special*. After all, that programme in his time was almost as much a celebration of friendship as it was of cricket. Every one of the team who has ever commented on the institution has gone out of his way to marvel at how, despite the disparity in background and temperament, there was never a cross word in the commentary box – no feuds, no disputes, only a spirit of mutual respect and amity, leavened (and made bearable!) by teasing, in-jokes and leg-pulls.

John Woodock, who knew Brian for almost fifty years, wrote in a *Times* tribute that he had never spent an unhappy day in his company. Trying or disappointing, perhaps, but unhappy no. 'There was a benevolence about him,' wrote Woodcock, 'that was truly infectious.'

As he pointed out, relations between the cricketers and the Press often, particularly in later years, became strained and lacking in trust. The arrival of Brian would change things.

'Wooders' wrote: 'Into the dining room or the foyer of the hotel he would come, making that ridiculous hunting horn noise of his which became a kind of signature tune and saying: "Hello, Cowders" or "Hello, Brearlers" or "Hello, Swanny" or "Hello, Godders" or "Hello, Unders" or "Wooders" or "Sir Geoffrey". Suddenly, the barriers would come down and things would start to look up.'

One of Brian's books was about his colleagues. It was called *Chatterboxes – My Friends the Commentators*. In the main the articles are as affable, friendly and urbane as you would expect, but once or twice the note changes. Coming from someone who sometimes seems to have devoted his lifetime to not causing offence, the lapses are surprising but they are there nonetheless.

I was surprised, for instance, when talking to E. W. Swanton at the Lord's Test in 1994, to hear Swanton say, 'Dear Brian. Wrote an awful lot of balls about me, of course.'

I was surprised because, without giving the matter a huge amount of thought, I had assumed that two such old school commentators would have been quite simply the best of friends. Perhaps so, up to a point, but Brian could be a terrible tease and, as sometimes happens with such people, he didn't always know when to stop.

In his appreciation of Swanton Brian wrote: 'Some people who don't know him think he is pompous. So, I suppose, do his many friends, which is why we enjoy pulling his leg.'

Brian did so consistently both in private and in public and sometimes with an edge.

Once around midday Jim announced that he would shortly be off for 'luncheon' in the committee room and asked whether Brian, whom he presumably regarded as the candidate best qualified to accompany him, would be coming too.

'No actually, thanks very much,' said Brian. 'I'm carrying my lunch with me. It's called a sandwich.'

Jim Swanton was even less amused by the stunt Brian pulled at Canterbury in 1963. When Swanton came on to do live commentary Brian and Co. waved a handkerchief as a pre-arranged signal to the players. Shortly afterwards the Kent captain, Peter Richardson, another keen leg-puller, went over to the umpire Bill Copson to complain about something. Play stopped and Copson walked to within shouting distance of the BBC position and called up, 'Could you please stop that booming noise. It's putting off the batsmen. Could you please stop it at once.' Colin Cowdrey, in the box that day thanks to a broken arm which prevented him playing, called back asking for a repeat of the message as they couldn't hear. By now the crowd realised what was happening and practically everyone in the ground except Jim was laughing loudly.

When Jim cottoned on he evidently said he supposed it was another of Richardson's silly tricks and we'd better get on with the game.

If anything he found it even less funny when Brian started to repeat this and other Swanton-puncturing stories in his writings and his after-dinner speeches.

There was another occasion on which Brian inadvertently caused offence to a friend. During a Test match there was a private lunch at Robin Marlar's at which Keith Miller, the great Australian all-rounder, revealed that he had recently undergone a prostate operation. That afternoon on *Test Match Special* Brian announced, with a chuckle, that Miller had had had the 'old man's disease'.

Apparently Miller was furious and upset by this but, having much of Brian's own attitude about unpleasantness and confrontation, decided it was best to let sleeping dogs lie. His old friend and sparring partner Denis Compton, however, took the cudgels up on his behalf and told Brian it was an invasion of privacy, hurtful to Miller personally and all sorts of things which Brian would have taken much amiss. Brian told Denis he was making a mountain out of a molehill, but the disagreement rankled.

It's odd in a way, because Brian was usually extremely anxious to avoid dispute or unpleasantness in the tight-knit team of cricket commentators and writers. 'He was not a critic,' says John Woodcock. 'He was seldom destructive or constructive. He was good-natured. He turned a blind eye to the bad in people.'

But his touch was not always sure even when he was trying to pour oil on the troubled waters.

David Frith, the knowledgeable but sometimes disputatious cricket pundit, told me how once he reviewed John Parker's sequel to Aubrey de Selincourt's classic novel, *The Cricket Match*. Frith didn't think much of the book and ended his piece with the triple expletive, 'Trite! Trite! Trite!' Brian was long associated with the magazine – he and Pauline were longstanding friends of its owner, Ben Brocklehurst, the former Somerset captain.

The next time Frith and Brian bumped into each other, Brian told him: '*We* don't write that sort of thing in *The Cricketer*.' It was the use of the word 'we' which irritated Frith almost as much as the rebuke. It implied that Brian was some sort of senior pro at *The Cricketer* and, as such, entitled to tell Frith, who after all was the editor, what was expected of him. Frith's rather punchy Australian outlook rebelled against this sort of assumption.

Brian did, however, have a clear idea of what constituted good form and correct behaviour, and although everyone I have spoken to agrees that he would never get too heavy about enforcing it, he would have no compunction in letting someone know if he thought they had got it wrong.

Despite that particular contretemps, in general the relationship between the two was never other than polite or cordial. It was not Brian's style to be anything else. Nevertheless Frith did think Brian plugged *The Cricketer* a little too shamelessly, particularly when, later, Frith ran a flurry of readers' letters in *Wisden Cricket Monthly* complaining about the facetiousness and frivolity of *Test Match Special*. This was considered by some – though not all – *TMS* insiders as being an unfriendly act.

There was, as nearly always with Brian, plenty of badinage

within the relationship. Frith recalls one occasion at Headingley when Brian was dying for a pee but found the door of the
official loo barred by a Leeds 'jobsworth' who refused to let
him in. Brian had no identity card and the guardian at the
gate refused him admittance. Frith on the other hand had a
press pass and was allowed to enter.

He vividly remembers a bursting Johnners hopping from
foot to foot, barely able to contain himself.

'Oh Frithers, Frithers, do tell him who I am!' he pleaded.

'Never seen him before in my life,' said a poker-faced Frith.
But he relented in the end and all was well.

It was Frith who told me a curious tale about about Brian
and John Arlott. After the death of Arlott's second wife,
Valerie, Frith was with Arlott in the library of the Old Sun, the
former Hampshire pub where he lived for many years before
retiring to Alderney. Arlott was beside himself with grief,
pacing up and down with the tears pouring down his face.
Then the phone rang and it was Brian calling to express his
condolences. Evidently all Brian was able to say was 'Poor
you! Poor you!' and this greatly upset Arlott. He apparently
considered it an inadequate and trivial response. As a rider to
this, however, Frith also told me that some years later, when
Arlott was in a terrible state and suffering badly, Brian had
reacted with much more eloquent concern and sorrow.

In a way I think the 'Poor you!' story may tell us as much
about Arlott as it does about Johnston, but there is no question
that relations between the two men were not exactly cosy.
They were always cordial, however, and when Arlott retired
they conducted a conversation on air which concluded with a
gracious tribute from Brian and an equally gracious thank-
you from Arlott.

Notwithstanding this, there was a widespread feeling in

cricket circles of there being an Arlott camp and a Johnston camp. Arlott could be grudging about Brian's jokes and general flippancy, his friends and followers even more so. It didn't help that Brian's postbag and general popularity were greater than Arlott's. It has been alleged that when Arlott retired from commentary he said, on leaving the box, that he had queered Brian's pitch by making it impossible for him to retire for at least three years – not that Brian seems to have had the slightest intention of retiring. And then there was the matter of drink. Brian enjoyed a glass of wine but only in moderation. Arlott introduced alcohol into the day's work, and though Brian would take a glass of Pouilly Fumé or champagne, I'm not sure he entirely approved. Once, and only once, he and Pauline went to Arlott's house for a meal, and Brian was apparently appalled by the amount of wine consumed. Arlott became considerably the worse for wear and Brian was unamused. He himself was such a controlled, well regulated personality that he disliked what he considered excess in others.

The other member of the team one might have thought Brian would have a prickly time with was Don Mosey, a.k.a. 'The Alderman' – so called because of a quiz programme Brian had once taken part in in Lancaster. Mosey was the producer and afterwards helped with the entertainment in the Mayor's Parlour. Brian thought he looked very Aldermanic and the name stuck.

Mosey is, on his own admission, a fully paid-up member of the awkward squad who delights in calling a spade a spade. He is also a professional North Country working-class lad, born in Yorkshire and living in Morecambe. He loathes privileged southern public schoolboys, and what he has written about *TMS*'s producer Peter Baxter and the *Telegraph* cricket correspondent Christopher Martin-Jenkins positively makes the toes curl. What he says about them in private is even worse.

But he adored Brian, even to the extent – like William Douglas-Home – of devoting an entire chapter to him in his autobiography. I went to see him in Morecambe and we spent some happy hours discussing Brian in the Morecambe Golf Club and later at the Mosey home. The settings were wonderfully unlike the ones one would associate with Brian – though I could imagine him doing a *Down Your Way* in the snug of the golf club as well as enthusing over Mrs Mosey's steak and kidney pie. The plain-speaking, chain-smoking Mosey simply didn't seem Brian's sort of person at first, and yet they plainly developed a rapport. Brian obviously appreciated Mosey's passion for sport; Mosey equally obviously loved Brian's generosity of spirit. And they shared a huge enthusiasm for competitive word-games. There was one in particular which almost became a private obsession.

I had told Mosey in advance that I wanted to explore this aspect of their relationship, and as soon as we had sat down in front of our pints at the club he produced a specimen sample. It consisted simply of a large square divided into smaller ones – five across and five down.

By the time the game had acquired a sort of national cult status, after copious mentions on *TMS*, Mosey had written out a one-side set of instructions on how to play. Before that, however, Brian had responded to queries on an *ad hoc*, one-to-one basis. He scribbled out a succinct message telling would-be players that they had to begin with twenty-five boxes and then build up as many words as possible by putting letters into each box. Players took it in turn to choose the letters and you scored ten for a five-letter word, five for a four, and three for a three.

One day he called Mosey in mild distress. He had received a letter from a listener saying that he had built his twenty-five boxes but was not quite sure how to proceed. The wretched fellow had painstakingly constructed twenty-five identical cubes, not realising that Brian's 'boxes' were no more than the sort of squares one scribbles for a game of noughts and crosses.

Mosey's specimen for me scored eighty points. The last word, left to right, was 'Truss'. 'Truss' was one of Brian's favourite word-game words. The other was 'Sewer'. 'Oh!' says Pauline, exasperated. 'All those S's!' She too was subjected to the word-game. Mosey used to tease Brian about 'Truss' and 'Sewer', saying that any man whose favourite words were these two had a problem. Brian enjoyed this. He was intensely competitive, always playing to win, which he almost invariably did. Mosey was inclined to experiment and play around with new constructions. Brian found a winning formula and stuck to it, with just the very occasional refinement. The game afforded this odd couple infinite enjoyment.

Mosey was as perplexed by his own liking and admiration for Brian as I was. It didn't really add up, and though we talked far into the night he never articulated his feelings more effectively than he did in his autobiography, *The Alderman's Tale* – even the title was a succinct tribute to Brian.

'One obvious explanation is, of course, that BJ [note that Mosey writes 'BJ', not Johnners] is one of the nicest people I have ever known – kind, generous, caring, wholly unselfish and unfailingly charitable. I have never heard him utter an unpleasant word about anyone in well over twenty-five years of our acquaintance. I have seen him actually *hurt* by the

vituperative outbursts of others, usually me ... A lovely
man, BJ. More than anyone or anything else in broadcasting,
I shall miss him.'

Others, many, have paid Brian that sort of compliment, but
I hope Mosey won't take it amiss when I say that, coming from
him, it is unexpected, and all the more convincing for that.

For Brian it often seemed that there really was 'nothing
worth the wear of winning but laughter and the love of
friends'. They came in many different guises, these friends,
though, uncannily, he managed to make all of them seem
special to him, whether they were predictable like the
Etonians and Grenadiers, quirky such as tykes like Mosey or
'Sir Frederick' Trueman, or, most bizarre of all, complete
strangers.

Over a year after his death Pauline had a letter from a chap
called Wrigley, whom she had never met, though he had
rented the family house in Swanage from time to time. His
story summed up this last category as well as anything I have
heard. It is an example of how Brian managed to become a
friend over the air, who somehow managed to engage,
console and reassure even though he was nothing more than a
disembodied voice coming out of the void from many miles
away.

'About twelve years ago,' wrote Wrigley, 'Mya and I were
travelling extensively and spent some time in India. We found
ourselves in a small town called Viorgil in Kashmir. An
unfriendly place – very Islamic, pictures of the Ayatollah
everywhere – just a stopover place on a two-day bus journey.
We were staying in a rather unsavoury, but cheap, hotel and
as it went dark our rather menacing hotel owner came down
the corridor towards our room. We were not feeling very
happy, rather wondering what on earth we were doing in such

a place, when I suddenly became aware of the transistor hanging from his hand. Sure enough, it was Brian Johnston from, I think, Trent Bridge – England vs Pakistan. BBC World Service! The menace disappeared and we had a cheery discussion about the alleged bias of English umpires! That very familiar voice from a long way away made us suddenly feel a lot nearer home.'

William Douglas-Home, Don Mosey and the Wrigleys in Kashmir, all in their different way were part of Brian's extraordinary gift of friendship. Such friendships were as important and fundamental to Brian as they were to his friends, and therein, I think, lies much of the secret.

13

A Question of Taste

What Johnners Liked

One of Brian's many signature tunes was a little ditty sung to the tune of the hymn, 'The Church's One Foundation'. The words go:

> She wears her silk pyjamas
> In summer when it's hot
> She wears her flannel nightie
> In winter when it's not
>
> And sometimes in the springtime
> And sometimes in the fall
> She'll slip between the bedclothes
> With nothing on at all.

The combination of *Hymns Ancient and Modern* with the mildest bawdy is typically Johnston. It has the same innocence as the vulgar Donald McGill postcards he so adored. 'She' sounds like the nubile junior matron, but you can't help feeling that if she did ask one of the boys between the bedclothes with her they would be deeply embarrassed.

One of his sons actually said to me, 'I don't think Dad was a terribly sexual animal.' Pauline, whose brother Gordon originally warned her, back in 1947, that Brian was 'a misogynist', says that he always liked blondes, which was as well for her when they met, as that's what she was. On their last cruise together Brian took a shine to a little fair-haired hoofer whom he christened 'The Smiler'. He would gaze at her dancing and smiling and befriended her, even writing on her behalf when she tried for work with the BBC.

Apparently it was all entirely innocent and Pauline raised no objections. Brian, for his part, never attempted to conceal his interest, and in this respect he and Pauline seem to have been unusually frank and open. Sometimes, on Sunday walks, they would compare notes, asking each other which of their friends or friends' partners they fancied. The answer, reassuringly and gratifyingly, was invariably 'none'.

John Woodcock, who was a boon companion on many overseas tours when the opportunities for dalliance were greatest, told me that if there was one man in the world who he would swear had always been completely faithful to his wife it would be Brian.

Not that he didn't have women friends. He was always close to Felicity, or 'Flossie', the sister of his old school friend, Jimmy Lane Fox. Shortly before they met she had contracted polio and was confined to a wheelchair. When he took her to the theatre, as he often did, Brian had to carry her about. This he did with aplomb, explaining to curious onlookers that she was 'drunk as usual . . . happens all the time'. This was a perfect example of his technique in such situations – how to

32. It's off to work we go.
Outside 1a Cavendish Avenue
with Pauline and Smokey.

Brian the tourist, photographed around the world by his friend and travelling companion John Woodcock.

33. With old friends Denis Compton (*left*) and Michael Melford, of the *Daily Telegraph*, at a country race meeting in South Australia, 1966.

34. Getting a good tip. Racing on the Savannah, Port of Spain, Trinidad, 1968.

35. Back in England. At the Dragon School ground, in Oxford, with Richie Benaud and Woodcock's spaniel Spinner.

36. Interviewing England bowlers John Snow, Robin Hobbs and David Brown on a Caribbean beach, 1967.

37. With Australia's former fast bowling terror Ray Lindwall at the 'Gabba', Brisbane, 1974.

38. Brian and friend photographed by Pauline in 1992 at Langa, near Capetown, home of the John Passmore Trust.

39. The *Down Your Way* team: sound engineer Brian Martin (*left*), Brian and producer Anthony Smith (*right*), with interviewee Chris Stevens.

40. The *Test Match Special* team in 1984. (*Front, left to right*) Don Mosey, Trevor Bailey, Brian, Freddie Trueman, Tony Cozier; (*back*) Tony Lewis, Henry Blofeld, Ray Illingworth, Christopher Martin-Jenkins, Peter Baxter and Bill Frindall.

Clothes for every occasion.

41. Receiving his OBE for services to broadcasting and cricket, 1 March 1983.

42. At the third Test, India vs England in Bombay, February 1993.

43. Interviewing Graham Gooch with Trevor Bailey during the fifth Cornhill Test, England vs West Indies at the Oval, 1991.

44. The end of a long day commentating on the third Cornhill Test, England vs Pakistan, at Old Trafford, 1992.

45. With Pauline, Mini and Edward Halliday's portrait, 1977.

46. The Johnston clan in the garden at Boundary Road, 1994.
(*Back row, left to right*) Barry with Olivia, David Oldridge (son-in-law),
Joanna, Ian, Andrew; (*middle row*) Fiona (daughter-in-law) with Sam,
Clare, Pauline, Gilly (daughter-in-law); (*front row*) Nicholas, Georgia,
Sophie, Emily, Harry, Rupert.

47. Relaxing on a hundred-year-old bench
bought from the Pavilion at Lord's, 1990.

defuse embarrassment or awkwardness by making a joke out of it.

In later years, when Flossie became a peer in her own right, Brian and Pauline often attended debates at the House of Lords and the three would dine together and talk politics. Brian enjoyed political discussion with Lady Lane Fox, not least because he agreed with her. If someone, such as Tony Smith, did not share his conservative views, politics became taboo.

William Douglas-Home claimed that Brian was once engaged to Elizabeth, daughter of their Eton headmaster, the famous Dr Alington. In Oxford, over dinner one day, William told Brian that she and his brother Alec had just announced their engagement.

'Well bless my soul,' said Brian, 'I was engaged to her myself last year at school.'

'Well, why didn't you marry her?' asked William.

'Because,' Brian replied, 'we were in the rhododendrons together one Sunday morning and Dr Alington walked by in his surplice on his way to Chapel and said "Come out of there, Elizabeth, you can do better than that." '

William conceded that in later years Brian claimed that he had never said any such thing but he insisted that 'my memory is not to be ignored'. Neither man, it has to be said, is an altogether reliable witness, and neither they nor Elizabeth are here to corroborate or deny. It carries the ring of at least some truth.

In Australia Brian always stayed with his former BBC colleague, the vivacious, bubbly Diana Fisher. She plainly adored him and remarked on what a creature of habit he was. Every morning she would make him his regulation breakfast with toast and marmalade and the morning paper. He would solemnly take the tray outside into the garden, consume the breakfast and the newspaper, and then be prepared to interact with other people. Diana said she always knew better than to engage him in conversation until after this ritual.

As one might expect, Brian always had an extremely good relationship with the secretaries who worked for him and typed his manuscripts, translating his difficult, sprawling handwriting. More than one came to regard him as a close personal friend. As always, he took a keen interest in people as individuals. It didn't matter whether they were grand Old Etonians or secretaries, housekeepers or footmen.

Women liked Brian because he made them laugh, because he had immaculate old-fashioned manners – at least in public – and because, while paying them attention, he was no sort of threat. Brian's own marriage was crucial to his life but he was often away from home. Even his wedding had to be timed to fit in with the cricket season. Then during all those years of *Down Your Way* he was away from home for an additional three days a week. After the Gillette Cup was instituted in the early sixties, with its final always played on the first Saturday of September, he was working through the whole of the summer holidays.

This meant that much of the bringing up of the children fell to Pauline. And the summer holidays for children at boarding school are the best opportunity sons and daughters have for getting to know their parents. She was anxious not to whinge – and if she did start to, Brian would say, 'You are lucky not to be married to a sailor!' He had always made it perfectly clear to her that he would be away a great deal and that in his absence she would have to cope as best she could. She had accepted this, but even so it had not always been easy.

Also that constant bonhomie and joking could become

wearisome. She remembered her father asking if 'that husband of yours ever says anything serious?' And there were occasions when she did slightly wonder. When he came into the house he wanted everyone to be happy, and his way of making everyone happy was to play games, tease, tell the old stories, do funny voices.

The trouble was that sometimes the making fun could become making fun of her. Brian had a habit of drumming his knife on the dining table while waiting for food to be dished up which maddened her, but this wasn't as bad as making jokes about the food when it arrived. She would have been slaving in the kitchen while the others played games or fooled around. Then, when the product of the steaming stove was put on the table, only for it to become the butt of Brian's humour, it was almost more than she could bear. It was worse still because the children joined in.

Finally she rebelled and the jokes stopped.

Part of the trouble was that he was a food-faddist *par excellence*. The basis of his taste seems to have been English school food, but even this is misleading.

Perhaps the single most unexpected revelation I uncovered about Brian is this.

'He didn't like cake.'

At least Pauline says he didn't like cake and they never ate it at home. Perhaps it was just that he got enough cake at work. He certainly enjoyed puddings like Spotted Dick and Treacle Sponge, though Pauline seldom cooked them because they were fattening. She says his favourite meal would have consisted of Heinz Cream of Tomato Soup; Scrambled Egg or Sardines on Toast; a Banana. He did love bananas and sometimes ate several in a day. He could be prevailed upon to eat an apple, but only if it was a Cox's orange pippin.

He loathed tomatoes with a passion since his illness in Brazil.

'I couldn't understand,' says Mrs Callander, alias Cally, the housekeeper and honorary family member, 'how he could hate tomatoes so much but loved Heinz tomato soup.'

Pauline says he once met Mr Heinz and complimented him on his tomato soup, telling him that what was so delicious about it was that it tasted of nothing like tomato. Mr Heinz was furious.

When Brian had food he loved he ate very fast – setting a bad example to the children, Pauline would complain – and always had seconds. But it wasn't just tomatoes he disliked. He wouldn't eat pork or shellfish; nor cooked cheese. In fact the only sort of cheese he could stomach even in an uncooked state was English Cheddar. Definitely no onions and no garlic. No beans – broad, round or even baked – and no carrots or courgettes. Preferably no sauces, though he liked Marmite with practically everything. Even fish pie. And of course he always followed the original pronunciation – 'Marmeat'.

This gastronomical fastidiousness dates back a long way, certainly, if his mother is to be believed, to his time in Santos, when his distaste for 'foreign vegetables' almost certainly brought on that debilitating illness. And it was an extreme aversion. Most of us have preferences about what we eat, and occasionally they are strong ones. Brian's, on the other hand, were wide ranging and expressed with peculiar vehemence. Confronted with a food he didn't care for he would not just swallow quickly and wash it down with a glass of water, or leave the room. Instead he'd spit it out with all the outrage of a man who had been poisoned.

Before a meal was served he would sometimes prowl round

the kitchen suspiciously lifting saucepan lids to check that nothing horrid like a broad bean or a tomato was being infiltrated without his knowledge. And if something incorrect did appear on his plate he could appear quite angry.

'You know how I only like flat mushrooms. How could you? How could you?'

It sounds a trivial matter but at times it imposed on Pauline a real strain. He was difficult to cater for and to cook for. Yet he never shopped, except for the simple things like bread and milk, and he never cooked, except for scrambled eggs at which he was a dab hand. I have a theory that many privately educated men of his generation were able only to cook scrambled eggs. But even so he was odd about eating and Pauline found it difficult.

Having put the case for the prosecution so roundly, I find myself feeling slightly guilty. Brian was perfectly well aware that he was considered, at least at home, to be fussy about food and offers a spirited, though not wholly convincing, defence in his book, *Someone Who Was*. He sounds quite cross when he says, 'I don't see why I'm said to be a fussy eater.' And although, in this passage, he doesn't once mention cake, he does insist, 'As for puddings I must be the easiest person ever.'

That's not entirely true but his taste on the pudding front is entirely predictable. His list of much-loved puddings begins: 'Roly Poly, Treacle Sponge and Tart, Spotted Dog, Bread-and-Butter Pudding . . .' It's no surprise therefore that his absolute all-time favourite, for which he even supplies his mother's recipe, is 'Guards' Pudding'. His version 'looks just like a Christmas pudding but is delightfully light and fluffy to eat'.

Oddly enough, many of the obvious cook-book writers make no mention of the dish. There's no Guards' Pudding in

my Delia Smith, Keith Floyd, Jane Grigson or even Mrs
Beaton. The only other recipe I could find was an old 1930s
one which Arabella Boxer reproduced in her anthology, *A
Second Slice*. Hers sounds less rich and less interesting than
Brian's.

In the interests of research I actually made it one day for a
family Sunday lunch. It was extremely easy and every bit as
good as he suggested.

You take:

> 6 oz fresh white breadcrumbs
> 6 oz chopped shredded suet or butter
> 4 oz brown or sand sugar
> 2 small eggs
> 1 level tspn bicarbonate of soda
> Pinch of salt

You mix all the dry ingredients except for the bicarb, then add
the wet ones beaten together with the bicarbonate of soda
and turn it all into a well greased mould and steam for three
hours. I mixed it all by hand, sensing that Brian's traditionalist
leanings would have preferred this to anything as new-fangled
and foreign as a Cuisinart or Magimix. He suggested serving it
with a frothy sauce of one egg, one yolk, $1^1/_2$ oz castor sugar
and two large tablespoons of orange juice, whisked up in a
bain-marie (though he would never have used such a fancy
word).

As far as I can ascertain, Brian would never have cooked
this himself. However, Guards' Pudding – and not, I'm afraid,
chocolate cake – was Brian's ambrosia. And his recipe strikes
me as being pretty foolproof. My family agreed with his

assessment and I shall include it in my repertoire, except that I shall rechristen it and describe it as 'Brian's Pudding'.

Brian was also quite fussy about hygiene and clothing. Often he would shave and bathe twice a day. On the few occasions that I met him I always noticed that he shone almost as if he had been scrubbed and polished. He was more than just clean, he was buffed like a Guardsman's boots.

'Just going to go and sponge my dock,' he used to say.

Clare says they were never actually told what his 'dock' was but they drew the obvious conclusion. When moving to and from the bathroom he tended not to bother unduly about nudity, even when he bumped into Mrs Callander.

Cally would put her hand over her eyes in a gesture of wounded innocence, and Brian would say breezily, 'Oops! Sorry Cally!' and hurry off to the sanctuary of the bedroom.

One day I asked Pauline about Brian and clothes. Many years ago I wrote a column for a glossy magazine about men's wardrobes. It was called simply 'A Man and his Clothes' and it was surprisingly revealing. I had no very clear thoughts about Brian's clothes beyond the extraordinary vivid brown and white 'co-respondent' brogues that he always wore during the Lord's Test match. Apart from that I had a vague impression of a conventional English toff's approach to clothes. I didn't think that he would ever have descended as far as odd socks, and he struck me as too fastidious to have soup or eggstains on his tie, but I didn't have an impression of serious sartorialism. My sense was that Etonians and Guardsmen of his generation would have thought that to give much attention to clothing was a bit effeminate or dandifyied. Not quite the thing.

I was wrong.

He bought the original pair of brogues in Port Said on his

way to cover an England tour of Australia, but from then on he always had his serious shoes – including two subsequent pairs of the famous brown and whites – hand made by a company called Barkers at Earl's Barton in Northamptonshire. For evening wear he favoured black suede brogues, also from Earl's Barton. Pauline opened the wardrobe and showed me several pairs, neatly lined up. For loafing around he liked to wear boating shoes or, latterly, string-drawn moccasins.

Although he was colour-blind he always liked to wear pale blue or yellow socks. He didn't like them too long but preferred them to come just above the ankle. He did not like elasticated socks, because they were too tight. On the other hand he did not use garters or suspenders. For years Pauline, who acted as his sock-purchaser, scoured the shops desperately looking for the elusive self-supporting, non-elasticated sock. Finally they resorted to getting them through a mail-order firm.

He sometimes wore polka dot or Union Jack underpants, which showed under his thin summer trousers.

When Pauline first married him he used to wear a Celanese vest underneath his shirts, which were often nylon. One day, without warning, he suddenly abandoned the vests. He was an extremely hairy-chested man, and Pauline thinks this may have something to do with the fact that he enjoyed the feel of soft fabrics next to the skin. Latterly he had taken to ordering hand-made silk shirts from the legendary 'Sam the Tailor's' in Kowloon. Manoo, son of Sam, remembers him with affection, though his cheques are not displayed under the counter of his shop like those of the Governor of Hong Kong, Chris Patten.

Because Brian had slim hips he tended to wear braces with his suits, which were usually from Aquascutum in Regent

Street. He had one tweed jacket and one dark blue blazer with Grenadier Guards buttons. Recently he had acquired a new set of these. After his old comrade-in-arms Charlie Sheepshanks died, his widow Mary sent Brian his old blazer buttons.

At home, relaxing, Brian, favoured an open-neck shirt, Daks slacks – before they stopped making them – and a variety of sweaters, often associated with cricket. That of the Riff Raff Club, for instance, of which he was President.

Pauline never gave him a tie because he was constantly being presented with ties by friends and well-wishers. The ties hanging in his wardrobe would practically make an exhibition at the Victoria and Albert Museum. The ones he particularly favoured were the vivid rhubarb and custard of MCC, the sober silver crowns on dark blue of Vincent's, the Oxford sporting club; those of the XL Club, the Primary Club (awarded to those who have at one time in their cricket career made a Golden Duck) and the Eton Ramblers. I was surprised that he did not wear the distinctive navy blue and magenta of the Guards nor the duck-egg stripes of his beloved Eton. But he was emphatically a man who, all his life, wore meaningful ties, whether crested or striped.

He was also a two-a-day handkerchief man. That large proboscis was frequently blown. The trusty Cally had to iron a minimum of fourteen handkerchiefs a week.

Is there anything to be deduced from Brian's clothes? I think I understand what Pauline means when she says that he wasn't really interested in his dress. She told me, for instance, that his colour-blindness led to him sometimes mismatching items of dress, so that he might appear in different coloured jacket and trousers when he was actually supposed to be wearing a suit. Certainly whenever I saw him he was very smartly turned out in the sense that everything was cleaned and ironed and polished. Those hand-made shoes suggest a note of showbiz – confirmed incidentally by his liking for extremely exuberant local shirts when touring in his beloved Australia or the Caribbean. There was one yellow number, picked up in Durban in 1967, which he wore on every single overseas trip thereafter. The hand-made silk shirts suggest a fondness for being cosseted. The penchants for light blue or yellow socks and polka dot underpants are a mystery.

His style of dress was certainly individual without – those shoes apart – being eccentric. I would say that he always dressed in a significantly more flamboyant manner than his brother Grenadiers, for instance. More conventional Guards officers of his generation, such as Lord Carrington or Lord Whitelaw, subscribe to an altogether more conservative code and have always seemed, by comparison, subfusc in appearance.

He was always well turned out on parade and would never have offended against the rules. But at the same time you could usually deduce from what he was wearing that this was a one-off figure with perhaps a foot in several different camps. Without ever being camp or outrageous, his clothes helped him cut a figure which was always noticeable and highly individual.

14

Happy Family
A Man for All Seasons

Public and private selves are seldom quite the same, and no man can ever seem quite the same to his wife and children as he does even to close friends, let alone to the world at large. Yet in the case of Brian he was extraordinarily accomplished at making casual acquaintances feel that they knew him inside out. In a curious way this makes life difficult for his family. It is almost as if he were such public property that they are denied their share of his private self. I am reminded of the child psychotherapist's phrase about his wanting to make the whole world his family. If that were at all true, where did that leave his family?

Barry, his eldest son, was born in 1949. Kenneth Thornton remembers being shown a photograph of the infant boy by the proud father who exclaimed to them, 'Looks just like a Buddha, doesn't he?' And to them, and other friends, 'Buddha' became Barry's enduring nickname.

Barry concedes that he was not the easiest teenage son and that the two only really got to know each other well after he had left school and gone into the music business and broadcasting. This gave them a common language and shared interests. When Barry's band, 'Design', played the Savoy Hotel, which Brian loved and where he used to stay during his war-time leaves, it was almost as proud a moment for Brian as seeing a son walk down the pavilion steps at Lord's. That was what he said, both to Pauline and to Barry, at the time.

'As a child I used to think he was the funniest person in the world,' Barry told me. 'He used to love to make us laugh.'

There was one day at prep school in Sunningdale when Brian took him and a friend out. In the car Brian kept up a string of jokes and word plays and puns which reduced Barry's friend to the sort of helpless laughter which followed Brian wherever he went. Practically every phrase or word produced a punning response: 'Summer pudding . . . or some are not . . . Intense . . . under canvas . . .' They may not look side-splitting, cold on the printed page, but anyone who remembers Brian's delivery and sense of humour will appreciate that when he came up with them, particularly when specially geared for small prep school boys on a day out, they were absolute bliss.

Brian's brother Christopher thinks that perhaps Brian tried too hard with the boy Barry. He remembers family visits to Berkshire when the car had hardly come to a halt before Brian had opened the boot, pulled out stumps and bat and ball, and told Barry to get padded up.

'If you want him to love cricket,' Christopher used to say, 'you have to make him *want* to play. Deprive him of it. Don't always allow him to play. Don't bounce him into it. That way he'll come to enjoy it.' But Brian couldn't understand how anyone, least of all a son of his, could fail to love the game just as he had always loved it. 'He overdid it,' says Christopher.

The pressure didn't pay – any more than when Christopher himself had been dragged out to play with Michael and Brian in Bude in the 1920s.

In the event Barry was at best indifferent to cricket. Almost as bad, he was indifferent to Eton. He didn't play games at the school, nor did he do any more work than he had to, preferring to stay in his room, smoking Gauloises and playing the guitar.

The Gauloises led to one incident which, for a time, seriously damaged Brian's faith in his Alma Mater.

The cigarettes were a serious tactical error because Barry's housemaster was a non-smoker, and the high-tar French cigarettes left a smell which was even more unmistakable than traditional English or American style cigarettes. Inevitably Barry was discovered and reported to the headmaster, the now controversial figure of Anthony Chenevix-Trench. Chenevix-Trench had a reputation, since confirmed in an official book, as a complicated man with an excessive relish for personally administered corporal punishment.

That evening Barry's housemaster came to his room and said that the headmaster wanted to see him in his private study. It was 10.30 – hardly a conventional time for an interview with the headmaster, much less a one-to-one session in his personal quarters.

Barry turned up, was ticked off about the Gauloises and told that it was a beatable offence and he must bend over. Barry duly flipped up the tails of his Eton jacket in the time-honoured manner and bent over. Chenevix-Trench advanced on him but instead of beating him he merely touched Barry's bottom with the palm of his hand. Barry can't remember, almost a quarter of a century after the event, whether it was a slap or a tickle or somewhere between the two. But it certainly wasn't a beating.

'Now,' said Chenevix-Trench, 'you've shown you are prepared to take your punishment like a man, so I'm not going to beat you.'

However, he was bound to tell both Barry's housemaster and his father that he had administered a beating, so he asked Barry to go along with the deception. He would write to the housemaster and to Brian telling them that the beating had taken place, and Barry was to confirm this.

After getting the headmaster's letter Brian had a private conversation with Barry. It was not his style as a father – nor in any other role – to express anger or to be confrontational. Barry remembers that his usual style was to gaze gloomily at the awful school reports and then look up at Barry with an air of troubled incomprehension. 'I don't understand, Barry,' he used to say. 'I mean couldn't you just try a little harder? It's costing an awful lot of money.'

This time, however, he was agitated and cross-examined Barry with more than usual vigour. After a while Barry felt the matter was getting out of hand and decided to own up to the truth.

Brian was even more appalled. 'Do you mean to say that the headmaster asked you to lie to me?'

Barry admitted that this was so.

It is difficult to be certain at this distance in time and without Brian here to explain, but my sense is that his reaction was not dissimilar to that which greeted John Profumo when he made his statement to the House of Commons about Christine Keeler. What really rankled with Brian was not Barry's minor fall from grace – after all had he not smoked

BDVs behind the fives courts at Temple Grove? Nor, though it exercised him, was it the eccentricity of the encounter's time and place. But for the headmaster of Eton to ask his son to lie to his housemaster and his father, this was beyond the pale. Brian wrote a furious letter to Chenevix-Trench and got a six-page handwritten letter of apology.

Family and friends agree that the episode shook Brian. For some time he even stayed away from Old Etonian reunions and dinners. Neither of his other two sons went to the school. It seemed to him that Eton had let itself down, that it was not the honourable place at which he had been educated. He hated what he perceived as a general decline in values and decency, and for Eton of all places to succumb to the trend was a bitter blow.

Once Barry's band was established the two 'became friends', though Barry still says that his father was not an easy man to have a very deep rapport with. Indeed in some ways he remembers him almost more as a 'jolly uncle' than a conventional father. Apart from anything else he wasn't around, which meant that Pauline had to be tough in order to get through the nitty gritty of family life. 'I remember,' says Barry, 'she would say, "Wait till your father gets home," but when he did come through the door, he'd tell us a joke.'

'He never talked religion. Or politics. He loved politics but he'd never debate it.'

Pauline even suggested that he might have taken up politics as a profession, but he would surely have hated the abuse, the intolerance and the painfulness of it all.

Christopher says he did once suggest Brian stood for Parliament.

'He said, "No. I couldn't stand the criticism." '

Generally Brian did everything he could to avoid confrontation, and would frequently nip arguments in the bud by saying, 'Let's compromise.'

'He didn't like talking about feelings,' says Barry. 'He found it embarrassing.' In the late seventies Barry went to California to try to crack the song-writing business. Brian was supportive as ever. Remembering, perhaps, his own not very happy years in the family coffee business, he was always adamant that his own children should be allowed to do what they wanted in their own way. He was also very proud of Barry's achievements and convinced that he would indeed become a great song-writer.

California at that time was the home of all touching, all expressive displays of emotion and affection, and Barry was moving in a culture quite unlike anything his father was familiar with. For Brian's seventieth birthday in 1982 he felt moved to send him a card telling him how proud he was of him and how much he loved him. Brian never acknowledged it nor mentioned it, but Pauline told Barry that he had tears in his eyes when he read it.

That same year was Brian's *This Is Your Life*. Andrew was in Australia at the time, but flew back home via Los Angeles where he picked up his elder brother. Although he was taken by surprise when Eamonn Andrews first revealed himself, Brian had discussed the possibility of being on the programme, and told Pauline that if it did happen and there were two prominent empty chairs he would guess that Barry and Andrew had been flown back.

So when Barry came in to the studio Brian managed to look pleased rather than flabbergasted and also had the presence of mind, when Barry gave him a restrained hug, to say out of the corner of his mouth, 'We don't kiss, do we?' (a question very distinctly expecting the question 'no').

'No,' answered Barry, quoting the old family joke, 'but Andrew's coming next and he's going to give you a big wet one.'

He then sat down and had the secret pleasure of watching Brian's apprehension as Andrew entered and advanced on him with lips poised. Mercifully he forbore.

There was a certain poignancy at the very end. Barry had been working in local radio (Sussex and Solent) but was casting around for a new venture. The idea of making a recording of 'An Evening with Johnners' involved BarryMour productions which he had set up together with his friend Chris Seymour. Within eighteen months of Brian's death the cassette sold more than 100,000 copies and won a gold disc. On the heels of this BarryMour has not only produced a tape of Brian's early escapades with *In Town Tonight* but is also expanding with cassettes from Ned Sherrin, Roy Hudd, Bill Pertwee and Donald Sinden.

It is a touching final legacy – an opportunity on the one hand to perpetuate Brian's voice and humour and on the other to lay the foundations of a new career for his elder son.

A funny thing happened when I went to see Brian's daughter Clare at her home in Balham.

I walked from the bus-stop and as I reached her front gate she was standing in the doorway. Just as I put my hand on the gate she let out a scream which made me jump a foot in the air.

This was unfortunate because when my left foot came down it landed in some wet paint on the pathway. She had had part of the path and the front steps painted that very morning. Her scream was designed to prevent me messing up the paint-work but had precisely the opposite effect.

Somehow, by letting her take my brief-case from the top of the steps and by her holding on to my hand and giving me a good yank I was able to gain entry without causing further damage. When the time came to leave, however, I had to jump down the steps to miss the paint again. I managed this all right but my landing was less than Olympic standard and I succeeded in planting a solid foot print in much the same spot by the gate as I had done earlier.

'Oh you are HOPELESS,' she cried out, brandishing my case in a mixture of mirth and irritation.

Like father, like daughter, I thought.

'If you say you'll do something then you must do it,' she had told me. 'If you didn't he got angry. I was always the efficient one. So he relied on me if there were questions about wills and powers of attorney, all that sort of thing.'

They used to have this private joke about punctuality. If they agreed to meet at, say, a restaurant at one o'clock precisely, then their footsteps would hit the doormat at precisely the same moment just as the clock struck one. Also she was the one child who was seriously keen on and good at games. She even played cricket. For years she would sit on the arm of his chair and help with the *Telegraph* crossword. And although he was away a lot she never felt he was absent, because every week there were letters or postcards from him no matter where he was in the world. He always called her 'Clara'.

When she was 22, Brian suggested Clare went to Australia, where she spent three very happy years running a tourist office for the French Pacific island of New Caledonia. Returning overland via South America, Clare then worked in public relations, and subsequently ran her own PR business after her marriage in 1980. Since 1989 she has worked on a part-time basis running Richie Benaud's UK office.

'I was devoted to my father,' says Clara. 'He always phoned about three times a week, either for a chat or to impart his latest joke. He also took immense pleasure in watching his eldest grandson Nicholas's progress at cricket, and I'm very sad that he can't be here to see him wicket-keeping for his prep-school's first XI.'

Andrew was the one he always played games with. 'Cards gentlemen please!' he would cry. No matter whether it was one of his favourite card games such as 'Chase the Ace' or a word game like 'Scrabble' or 'Boggle', he was always intensely competitive. Andrew's mistakes or shortcomings were inevitably greeted with derisive snorts and shouts of 'Silly ass!'; his own triumphs were given such accolades as 'There you are – "Boggle Champion of the World".'

Like Barry, Andrew says that he only really got to know Brian well in adulthood. Partly because of Brian's disillusion with his old school and partly because Andrew so hated boarding, he went to Westminster. But even so, Brian was away a lot.

Even when he was at home I have a sense that, with Andrew too, Brian was often a slightly perplexed parent. There was no shortage of affection, but he had no role-models to guide him except the distant father he barely knew and the raffish Scully who usurped him. Andrew recalls one poignant moment when he was about seven years old and asked Brian if he would teach him to fish.

Brian did not have the first idea about fishing but recognised that it was part of a father's duty to teach a son such things. The most rudimentary rod and line was therefore assembled – little more than a stick and a length of string – and the two set off up the hill to the round pond on Hampstead Heath. There a worm was transfixed on to the pin at the end of the string and little Andrew was instructed to dangle it in the water. Then they sat for what seemed a long, long time. Nothing whatever happened. Occasionally Andrew would turn to his father and ask if he was doing it right. Every time he asked, Brian replied that he was doing absolutely fine.

Then, eventually, Brian said that perhaps it was time they both went home, so Andrew withdrew the worm from the water and the two set off back to St John's Wood.

And that was fishing.

Their relationship really matured years later when, after a spell with Foyles the booksellers – where he achieved some spectacular successes selling his father's books – Andrew went to Australia to work in publishing. He eventually stayed there for twelve years before returning to England in 1987. To see something of the country on the cheap he bought himself a camper van, and when Brian was commissioned by the BBC to tour Australia for a series of 'Down Your Way Down Under' he installed an armchair in the back in which to drive his father around in style. Brian's producer Tony Smith accompanied them from Sydney to Wagga Wagga, Canberra, Adelaide and latterly Melbourne. It was there that Andrew remembers the only time that he had seen a joke backfire on his father, who had been introducing him (at six foot four) to all as 'my little boy'. They went to see the England Women's Cricket team playing at a small ground outside Melbourne and Brian ordered 'one and a half' tickets from the gate as a further tease. He was amazed when these were duly given, and when he owned up to really wanting two adult tickets he was told, 'No, you're right mate, it's full price for adults and half price for old age pensioners.'

Of all Brian's children it is the youngest son, Ian, who looks, and sounds, most like him. He has the same solid style as his father and has even inherited his habit of christening people with those familiar nicknames usually ending in 'ers'. He was born in 1957 and, because of *Down Your Way* and *Test Match Special*, Brian possibly missed more of his childhood than any of the others'.

Ian has always had a mania for travelling and went off to Australia as soon as possible after leaving school at Bradfield. Like his brothers, he disliked school and longed to be footloose and free. At various times he has worked for Our Price records, as Manager of a night club in Henley and General Manager of a cable TV company. His latest job is with Channel One, though he has also found time to be the driving force behind the Brian Johnston Memorial Trust, designed to raise £5 million for such varied causes as young cricketers, old actors, the blind and village cricket. John Paul Getty is the patron and John Major one of the vice-presidents.

Sadly Ian was travelling in South America when Brian suffered his heart attack, and only learned of his death two days after the funeral.

Joanna, the youngest, was born in 1965, when Brian was already 53. Sadly she was born with Down's syndrome and now lives in a special community for the mentally handicapped in Hertfordshire, though she often visits home in Boundary Road. Hers is a mild form of the condition and she is technically 'a Mosaic'. This meant that in everything she did she had a fifty per cent chance of improvement. She would never be able to lead a completely independent normal life, but she would be able to acquire skills. And so she has. She sews proficiently, plays the piano and, above all, has developed a distinctive style of abstract painting which is so successful that her work has been exhibited in London galleries. Pauline has several on the walls of the drawing-room at Boundary Road. They're bright, cheerful, unusual and very pleasing. Brian would have been proud of them, as he invariably was of all her achievements, particularly as they were hard-fought against difficult odds.

Characteristically, he made relatively light of this 'bit of bad luck' as he called it, and even, in *Someone Who Was*, left Pauline to tell the story. There was no lack of love or concern on his part, but he found it difficult to talk about such things in public. The former Archbishop of Canterbury, Robert Runcie, also a war-time Guards officer with an MC to his name, remembered how Pauline was anxious to arrange for Joanna's confirmation in a Hertfordshire parish church, which Runcie, as the former Bishop of St Albans, knew all about. It was not a complicated request. It simply meant the Archbishop having a quiet word with the rector. He was happy to do so, and in the end the event passed off happily. Brian was duly grateful and said a sincere thank-you.

However, Runcie says that it was very noticeable that when Pauline made the original request Brian stayed in the background and remained silent. He formed the impression that Brian was an Englishman of the kind who believed that talking about religion and other such matters was best left to the women. He felt that there might have been a whole area of Brian's emotional life which was kept carefully suppressed.

Certainly Joanna remembers Brian with the same sort of love tinged with just a measure of exasperation which characterises the rest of his family. When I asked her about her father she talked about going to the theatre and being introduced to famous people backstage after the show. She particularly mentioned meetings with Princess Ann and Jason Donovan which seem to have been the two high spots. He always used to tease her and this was done affectionately. But just occasionally he would overstep the mark. He used to call her 'Joey', which she didn't like.

From the first he and Pauline wanted her to be treated as normally as possible. Pauline started a little nursery group in the church hall; then, when the teacher left, they sent her to a small nursery school with a teacher, called Mrs Williams who wrote rhyming couplets about the cleaning of teeth, the pet dog and crossing the road. Barry set some of these to music and made a record of them. After that they took on a retired teacher, Vyvyan Jenkins, who came to the house twice a week and taught Joanna to read and write. As a result of this, when she moved on to a Montessori School in Primrose Hill she was actually more advanced than some of her 'normal' contemporaries.

While here it was discovered that she had diabetes. This was a grim time. Brian was away. Pauline was flat on her back with disc problems. Great Ormond Street and the famous and indefatigible 'Sister Mac' performed wonders. Later Joanna was a star guest in Sister Mac's own *This Is Your Life*. Nevertheless there is no doubt that despite the rewards of Joanna's loving personality these were difficult moments.

A year or so later she went to a pioneer school in Bethnal Green where there was a mixture of handicapped and normal children. This involved a daily half-hour car journey to Islington, where she picked up the school bus. Whenever possible Brian would chauffeur her and use the time to indulge in jolly learning exercises – spelling games, question and answer sessions in French, and her multiplication tables – learned in much the same way as Brian would have learned them at Temple Grove.

In her early teens Joanna went to board at a PNEU (Parents' National Educational Union) school called Flexford House near Newbury. She thrived and progressed but there were always set-backs. At home she frequently went walk-about, and the St John's Wood police became quite used to Mayday calls from Boundary Road saying that Joanna had gone absent without leave. On one occasion she saw a television advertisement which told viewers to dial 999 if they wanted the police in an emergency – and did just that. The first Pauline and Brian knew about it was when they found her coming downstairs from her bedroom with two uniformed constables. She had let them in on the entryphone.

Later they were offered a place for her in a new home opened by the Home Farm Trust near Biggleswade in Hertfordshire. Then about a year after Brian's death she moved into one of the Trust's houses in Biggleswade itself. There she would have more independence and be able to do her own shopping. One feels that Brian, who seems to have been at the same time immensely protective but also anxious that Joanna should enjoy as much independence as possible, would have approved.

She is a religious person and draws solace from her faith. She was confirmed just a month before Brian's death. At her neck she wears a crucifix and from time to time she will finger the little cross and smile and say, 'I've got my Dad here inside me.'

At the time of his death Brian had seven grandchildren – an

eighth was to arrive shortly after. He enjoyed them with a pleasure made still greater because it was uncomplicated. He could simply amuse them, play games with them and watch them grow up. Best of all, some of them, unlike his own sons, were good at cricket. When Nicholas, the eldest, got the cricket 'bug' at the age of three, Brian had equipment specially made for him. Later the boy even showed signs of being seriously good and was singled out for special praise by the MCC coach, Clive Radley. Brian purred.

When he wrote or talked about his family Brian always had a mention for Mrs Callander, alias Cally or occasionally 'Callybags' ('Not so much of the "Bags",' she would say when thus addressed). Cally came to the Johnstons in answer to an advertisement in the *Lady* in 1960, and has been with them ever since. At the first of their two St John's Wood family homes she lived in, having her own flat. At Boundary Road there is no accommodation for her, but she is still a regular presence, and as much a part of the family as anyone who is not a blood relation can ever be.

Before Pauline and Brian met, her brother Gordon told her that Brian probably wouldn't be interested in her, and Brian himself conceded that, at the time, he was a happy, possibly 'confirmed' bachelor with little 'time or inclination for the opposite sex'.

In the end of course they were together for forty-six years and nothing suggests to me that Brian ever found it a day too much. There were tiffs and discrepancies. Pauline says she was more interested in the arts than he ever was. And whereas he was a master of punctuality, she was nearly always late. Brian was strenuously polite and emollient; Pauline, in an old Yorkshire tradition, is sometimes inclined to call a spade a spade. This too sometimes gave rise to gentle friction. Food, as we have seen, was often a source of mild dispute – or jokes which weren't as funny as they were meant to be.

But what is this in half a lifetime of marriage?

Pauline herself is almost as understated as Brian would have been. 'We kissed each other every morning and night and whenever either of us left the house,' she said, 'but we never said "I love you" like they do in America all the time.'

All very English. Like everything else about Brian. But under no circumstances to be discounted because of that. Theirs was a long partnership and a happy one according to all those most intimately involved. I think Pauline was right. They might sometimes have seemed to outsiders to have been oddly matched. But outsiders never understand.

Pauline considers they made a good team. Brian said they were simpatico. Their children concur.

15

I Say, I Say . . .

A Night on the Road

Throughout his life Brian mined his experiences in the cause of entertaining others and making them laugh. He was a fine imitator and anecdotalist who was telling funny jokes and stories from his earliest days. In 1952 he wrote his first book, based on 'Let's Go Somewhere', and produced a steady stream thereafter. Some, such as two volumes about *Down Your Way*, are based on radio days. Others, such as *The Wit of Cricket*, and *Brian Johnston's Guide to Cricket*, are founded on his best loved game. *It's Been a Lot of Fun*, *It's a Funny Game* and *Someone Who Was* are more generally autobiographical.

As the titles suggest, the books are fun. Sometimes the amusement is a touch wry – the title for the last was prompted by the remark of a woman who met him on Paddington Station and said, 'I think I recognise you, don't I? Aren't you someone who was?' This must have prompted a rueful grin. But in the main the books are as breezy as the man himself.

The written word, however, was never his true *métier* and he was happier with the spoken. Not for nothing was the child Johnston called 'The Voice'. For years he was in demand as an after dinner speaker and told his favourite jokes and stories with aplomb and panache and sometimes invention. His sometime publisher, Geoffrey Strachan of Methuen, recalls a virtuoso performance at the National Theatre. In *Someone Who Was*, Brian had rearranged his life into alphabetical sections from 'A for Actors and Actresses' to 'Z for Zany' (he was obviously a little non-plussed by 'Z'). Before a live audience of seven hundred, Brian, noteless and fearless and never glancing at his watch, waltzed through his life's alphabet without a pause in precisely forty-five minutes -- the alloted time. A virtuoso performance.

This gift reached its ultimate refinement at the very end of his life when he put together a one-man show which was not only an idiosyncratic summary of his highly individual life, and the summit of his ambitions, but also a theatrical achievement to set beside those of his salad day heroes of the music hall. The performance is *sui generis*, the gospel according to Brian, and an Old Age Pensioner's triumph. In many ways it represents the sum of his parts, but it is also, I think, in many ways, the most extraordinary thing he ever did.

In a sense this was what he had always wanted to do. At last it was as if he were his own one-man Crazy Gang, up on the stage in front of a live audience, telling his favourite old jokes and stories, playing tape recordings of one or two of the better known pranks and even managing a bit of a croon. Oh my Flanagan and Allen long ago, long ago!

His old friend 'Wooders' went to see the show in Salisbury and was appalled when Brian sat down on his high stool in front of a packed house at the Playhouse and embarked on his opening joke. 'Wooders' buried his face in his hand. He had been hearing these lines regularly since 1948.

'He can't tell that one,' he said to himself, 'he simply can't.'

But then to his amazement Brian got to the punch-line, delivered it with that familiar chortle and was received with rapturous applause. 'Wooders' realises now that there was no cause for alarm. That infectious small boy legerdemain had triumphed again. It was the same indefinable something which had reduced him to stitches when he had tried to record that radio interview all those years ago. It had gone on making him giggle ever since and, mysteriously, it had the same hypnotic effect on a live audience of several hundred as it did on one.

I never saw the show, but like thousands of others I have the tape that Barry made at Canterbury a few months before his death. It is worth dwelling on because, in a sense, it is Brian's life digested into an easily absorbed couple of hours and presented in his own inimitable, but sometimes deceptive, manner.

How did it work, that Johnston magic?

I have spent hours listening to the tape recordings of that last-of-the-summer-wine 'Evening with Johnners' and staring at his face, captured in a photograph of Pauline's on the front of the cassette. The voice never really did grow old, but the picture is definitely that of an elderly gent. The white hair is very thin, the eyes look slightly rheumy, with tufty sea-lion eyebrows fringing them and wrinkly bags below. The smile is humorous all right, but am I alone in detecting a rueful quality to it which would not have been apparent a few years before? It's a clever photograph, however, because it manages to make Brian appear to be looking straight at you – through you even – with just that expression of complicity which was one of his gifts. Whatever thought he is thinking, he wants you to feel that it is shared. He reminds me of a benign old tortoise – been

191

there, seen that, had a lot of fun, not all a piece of cake but you and I understand each other, don't we? Well disposed, certainly, but with just the touch of melancholy they say attaches to all good comics.

He comes on stage to the strains of Haydn Wood's 'Horse Guards, Whitehall', the signature tune of *Down Your Way*, which the BBC, to his annoyance, had dropped after his departure. The march, obviously familiar to an audience who knew and loved the programme, is entirely right for him – perky, comforting and terribly English. It also has a hint of brassy oompah-pah which suggests music hall and variety. After a few bars the applause begins and if you close your eyes you can visualise him entering left and making his way to the solitary stool on stage. (It's now in his study in St John's Wood.)

He doesn't quite give his trademark hornblow, but there are some mild trumpetings before he manages to articulate, 'Thank you. Thank you very much and how nice to be in Canterbury. And how nice to see the names Huddle and Freeman on the sports shop just as I came to the theatre.'

This is deft professional stuff. There's nothing worse than hearing some tired old performer who has no idea where he is. I suspect Brian didn't go anywhere near Huddle and Freeman on his way to the theatre. He would have remembered it was the local sports shop and he would have taken the trouble to make sure they were still in business.

Now comes the first joke:

'I have to admit this . . . I had to stop just now saying "Hello Canterbury" . . . I've got in this terrible habit . . . wherever I am, it can be Bournemouth, Manchester, Birmingham, I say hello to the town, you see, and I've got to be very careful because next week I'm going across to the Isle of Wight and

I'm speaking to the ladies' luncheon club at Cowes . . . I've got to be a little bit . . .'

The end of the sentence is drowned in the first gust of gratifying laughter. 'Cowes' had been given an emphatic signpost and the audience had understood what he was saying. Not terribly difficult. Nor, on paper, terribly funny. Indeed it was the Johnston chortle which came immediately afterwards which seems to have made them laugh almost as much as the corny joke itself. 'Laugh and the world laughs with you . . .'

Then he tells the joke about last night's speech. There was this drunk who came up to him and said that it was the most boring speech he'd ever heard in his life, whereupon the chairman, not hearing what he had actually said, took Brian on one side and told him, 'Don't worry about him, he only repeats what everyone else is saying.'

More laughter. Putting yourself down is a sure-fire winner. No one in the audience will believe that this really happened to Brian, much less the previous evening, but he uses it to explain that he's feeling rather diffident about this evening and if he seems nervous this is why. He sounds – and I'm sure looks – utterly self-assured, but this is an effective way of winning your audience round, though this audience is very obviously on his side already.

'Marvellous to see so many people . . . I don't know . . . must be a very bad night on the telly or something.'

Another appreciative ripple. Other broadcasters have remarked to me that Brian often broke one of the first rules of public speaking, which is always to complete your sentence. He, however, was the past master of the phrase left hanging in the air. Since everyone always knew how his sentences were going to end, it didn't matter that he didn't always finish them.

And there's no doubt that it made him sound more natural and conversational.

Then comes the story about his friend who spoke to an audience of only one chap. (Most men in Brian's stories are 'chaps'.) When he'd finished he said to the one-man audience that he was now leaving, to which the chap replied, 'Please don't go – I'm the second speaker.'

'Oi!'

But they laughed.

A brief pause and then the theme for the evening. 'How lucky I am and how much fun I've had . . . wonderful family . . . mother and father . . . sister and two brothers . . . how close we've always been . . . that was great.'

Eton scores two anecdotes. There's the William Douglas-Home one when he is confronted with an exam paper which asks him to write as succinctly as possible about (a) Socialism and (b) Coal. To which the playwright answers with the single word 'Smoke'.

'He got ten out of ten, which wasn't bad.'

The other story was the Anna May Wong joke. House-master, infatuated with famous Chinese star; phone rings; senior boy (Martin Gilliat, later the long-serving major-domo at the Queen Mother's Clarence House) answers; returns looking doleful: 'Sorry sir, Wong Number.'

Did it ever happen? I doubt it. But who cares?

On stage Brian mumbled Gilliat's name, on the grounds perhaps that his audience might not have recognised it, and sums up, fast, 'That was Eton . . . then there was Oxford where I read History and P. G. Wodehouse . . . played cricket six times a week.'

Then the story of scoring the try in the macintosh. And that was Oxford.

Eton Two, Oxford One.

Then comes coffee, which rates one anecdote – the one with the office manager ticking him off for not being in at nine-thirty. This scores agreeably high on the laugh scale but quickly makes way for the Grenadiers ('Best regiment in the British Army'). He kicks this off with the story of the commanding officer welcoming a new subaltern with enticing tales of drink and sex. The words are much the same as usual, except that Brian has decided to attribute the incident to a friend of his who had just joined the Hampshire regiment in Sherborne. Apart from being an unwarranted slur on a respectable old county regiment, Sherborne is in Dorset, so Brian's 'friend' would presumably have joined the Dorsets. It doesn't matter. It gets a laugh, but it's another good example of trying to pretend that an obviously ancient chestnut is a true story. No one believes it, but somehow it makes the antiquity of the joke more palatable. The laughter suggests the ploy is working.

'Only speak if you can add to the picture,' he says before telling his audience about the Queen and Prince Philip returning from a tour of Australia in 1954 and how Brian and Richard Dimbleby planned their relative tasks. Dimbleby was on Westminster Pier waiting for *Britannia*, so they agreed he would paint a picture of the children with their Union Jacks, the Queen Mother, the corgis, 'Lord Lieutenants – all these sort of people, y'know' . . . (He likes to slip in 'y'know' from time to time, partly as verbal punctuation and partly because it increases the sense of complicity which is vital to this show's success.) After the Royal couple had disembarked, Dimbleby kept up his commentary, following the Irish State Coach halfway down the Mall where, metaphorically speaking,

195

Brian picked it up with a detailed description of the said coach, its history, size, appearance and so on.

'And so the great day arrived . . .' The trouble was the Queen was late; Dimbleby was lost for words and to his horror Brian heard him say, 'So as she hasn't arrived yet I'll tell you all about the Irish State Coach.' Which he did. Thirteen tons, given to Queen Victoria, solid gold . . . 'All that sort of thing.' ('All that sort of thing' is another of his conversational tics. In other commentators the phrase might be considered sloppy, but somehow it fits Brian like a glove.) Still the Queen hasn't arrived, so Dimbleby starts to describe the horses, one by one in detail. (Brian is spinning this story out, giving it much more detail and depth than the earlier staccato gags and one-liners.) 'I was going mad by now.' He had nothing left to say. So when Dimbleby handed over to him, as planned, half-way down the Mall, he remained virtually mute.

'And do you know, the next day people said to me, "You did the best television commentary I've ever heard. Better than Richard Dimbleby." And I realised why, because when they came past me I watched them . . . and they went past me, and I watched on my monitor as they drove into Trafalgar Square, turned left under Admiralty Arch, went about two hundred and fifty yards up the Mall, and as they approached Buckingham Palace I said, "Over now to Barclay Smith in Buckingham Palace".'

Huge laughter and applause.

'That's all I said, well, but what else could I say?' asks Brian through the clapping. 'They knew the Queen, they knew Prince Philip, they knew the horses, they knew the escort, they knew all about the Irish State Coach . . . so that was the lesson which I don't think many people follow nowadays. They perhaps talk too much, but there we were, that was that. And I learnt another thing from that television time . . .'

These stories are not unfamiliar – at least to me and to serious Johnston fans – but he tells them amusingly with enough colour to transport the listener back to the early fifties and those grand ceremonial occasions in the streets of London when the voices of men like himself and Richard Dimbleby really did seem to speak to the nation in the muted mellifluous tones of the officer class which was what the BBC was all about. John Birt wouldn't have got past the commissionaire!

He spends quite a lot of time talking about the differences between radio and television, about interviewing techniques, the signals given by studio managers. He lifts the veil a little, explaining arcane bits of broadcasting jargon and always injecting little bits of colourful anecdote spiced with corroborative detail – talking about the jet engine at an exhibition in the Horticultural Halls, the first match of the 1952 Indian cricket tour in Worcester and interviewing Mr Gupta ('Are you a selector?' 'No, I'm a Christian'), Uffa Fox at the Boat Show and coping with his French wife ('Only three things worth doing in life – eating, drinking and making love – and if you talk during any of them you're wasting your time').

We have only been going a few minutes and yet already, it strikes me, we have covered an enormous amount of ground, dropped an almost Nigel Dempsterish quantity of names and elicited a gratifying lot of laughter. There are critics of Brian who suggest that he was all charm, veneer and froth, but on the evidence of the evening so far, he scores surprisingly high on content. What's more, the jokes aren't just jokes for jokes' sake in the manner of some after-dinner speakers and stand-up comics; they are, most of them anyway, jokes and anecdotes which illustrate the point he is trying to make.

Nothing in the performance is particularly profound, but then why should it be? – it's an entertainment, not a sermon.

Now come famous mistakes – first Henry Douglas-Home, the nightingales in the grounds of Hever Castle and the girl saying 'If you do that again Bert I'll give you a smack in the kisser' (there *is* something inherently funny in the voice of Brian chortling out 'smack in the kisser'); and second, lying under the train outside Victoria station when the loo flushed. (People laugh inordinately when Brian says 'washing their hands' with a naughty Max Miller inflection and what I imagine is a naughty-boy expression which tells you exactly what he really means.)

Wynford Vaughan-Thomas, the *Ark Royal* and the Queen Mother; Robert Hudson and the Queen at Lord's; Brian himself at the Prince of Wales's wedding, when he said 'Up the steps into the pavilion' when he should have said 'cathedral'; John Snagge stories involving HMS *Vanguard*, Len Hutton – 111 not ill, Lord Reith and the copulating couple, and, of course, the Boat Race; Max Robertson and the Queen of Norway; Audrey Russell and the Queen's 'dark black'; Stuart Hibberd and 'interlush with Ernest Lewd'; Henry Riddle and the Queen going round the bend; the Queen Mother, Princess Margaret and the boil on the bum in the hospital ward; the farting of the Queen's horse during the State visit; Brian on stage with the Crazy Gang; singing 'Underneath the Arches' with Bud Flanagan; sucking a lemon with Jimmy Edwards; the interview from the pillar box; being hypnotised (a rare absence of laughter); 'How's your uncle?' on the steps of the Criterion Theatre.

The voice is beginning to sound a bit tired by now, so it's a relief to pause while he plays a medley of tapes of 'Let's Go Somewhere' compiled by Barry. This consists of the bareback riding at the circus, being turned upside down by the blonde lady at the Chiswick Empire, the motorbike ride with 'Mad Johnny Davis', the rather tardy relighting of the Piccadilly illuminations in 1949 – 'they had to repair all the things, I think'.

And so to *Down Your Way*, with a sudden note of near seriousness: 'A great programme to do though, this, because, you read in the papers, quite seriously about awful things like famine and rape and bombings and all the stuff that goes on round the world, but if you came round Great Britain with me, as I did for fifteen years, you realise still what a *marvellous* nation we are. Everybody, in every place, seemed to be doing things for other people . . . all these people doing things for other people and it didn't get in the papers, ever. It's good news but it doesn't. So we are still a marvellous nation and I was very lucky to meet so many of 'em.'

This is the nearest, during the evening, that Brian ever comes to philosophising, and, even if, on the page, it might have a sugary look, it is very much the heart of Brian speaking. This notion of everybody doing as they would be done by was what he most earnestly believed, and you feel, listening to him, that the sentiment encompassed that night's audience – so that even if, in reality, they were the most gruesome bunch of misanthropes and ne'er-do-wells, they were briefly transformed by Brian's magic wand into the ultimate good neighbours.

From the pudding of *Down Your Way* he picks such plums as the hundred-year-old Mrs Emily Brewster complaining that her telegram from the Queen was not in her own handwriting, and the muleteer from Usk who grew mustard and cress in his gumboots while out in India. And finally another tape recording, this one, typically, a piece of giggling – Richard

Booth, the uncrowned king of Hay-on-Wye, completely unable to articulate his musical choice of 'Golden Years or anything by David Bowie' – inexplicable but entirely infectious. And then, quite briskly, Brian says that there is now an interval of twenty minutes after which he will return to talk about 'a game called cricket'.

And so he does.

There goes that theme again and in he saunters with a breezy 'Oh . . . er . . . thanks for coming back', as if he was surprised that anyone had. From the volume of applause we may deduce that the house is still full.

'Just before we talk about cricket,' he begins, 'may I tell you a story about the Pope – do you mind?' He doesn't give anyone time to object, but launches into a very old story indeed about the Pope being diverted to Shannon airport by cross-winds and subsequently being arrested for speeding at the wheel of Paddy Murphy's white Rolls-Royce. It is quite a time in the telling but the punch-line, 'He must be a very important man – he's being driven by the Pope', was as successful as any that had gone before.

And so to 'lovely people like Peter West' and 'dear old Denis Compton'. He does the number about Denis celebrating his fiftieth birthday only to receive a phone call from his mother telling him he was only forty-nine.

He glosses over the sacking from television though he makes no bones about being sacked, admitting that 'they got fed up with all my bad jokes and thought they'd get in some Test players to do the commentary which was very sensible – they do it marvellously', and then concentrates on *Test Match Special*. Much predictable emphasis on 'fun', importance of having same. Then thumbnail sketches of colleagues coupled with anecdotes. Poor old Swanton is pilloried for pomposity as usual. Brian tells his audience that when, on *Desert Island Discs*, Roy Plomley asked if he'd cope on the island. Jim replied, 'Depends who the Governor-General was.' And follows it up with a chauffeur joke, the 'booming noise' joke, and the election of Swanton as pope joke. Poor old Swanton, a Kentish man after all. One rather hopes he hadn't made the journey from Sandwich to be in Brian's audience. John Arlott gets a mildly disingenuous eulogy – 'unique and we miss him terribly' – and a surprisingly good imitation as Brian delivers his verdict on the bowling action of Asif Masood ('reminds me of Groucho Marx chasing a pretty waitress'). Henry Blofeld comes in for some bus jokes and some gaffes. The Bearded Wonder is included in a very curious story about dressing up as an Arab, and a decidedly racist story involving Arabs in Golders Green is attributed to Fred Trueman.

A few moments discussing 'cake' without, it seems to me, enormous enthusiasm. 'It is rather stupid but people are kind and when people are kind you say "thank-you".' Reading between the lines, that says quite a lot on the knotty subject of confectionery and baking. The running cake gag, he almost, but not quite, concedes, did get slightly out of hand.

I'm not quite sure how we get on to the joke about the judge not quite hearing the defendant who said 'Sweet F.A.' when asked if he had anything to say before being sentenced. ('He definitely said something,' says the judge, when Counsel solemnly repeats the words. 'I saw him move his lips.')

And when it comes to bishops there is hardly even a pretence of a sequitur, just Brian saying, 'Bishops, what about bishops?' before doing the two bishops and pre-marital sex. ('I never slept with *my* wife before marriage, what about you?' To which the other bishop responds, 'I'm not sure. What was her maiden name?')

Of course Brian is being outrageously digressive, but who cares? Certainly no one in this audience. They're having far too good a time – as, from the manifest enjoyment in his voice, is Brian.

He pretends for a minute or two to be quoting from letters received in the commentary box. Perhaps so. But why pray should anyone write to *Test Match Special* in order to ask, 'What's a Frenchman called who's shot out of a cannon? Answer, Napoleon Blown Apart.' If people do send in these jokes the real reason must be that, unlike the recurring cakes, Brian so obviously adores them. Like the old lady knitting in the fast lane of the motor-way who is accosted by the police. 'Pull over,' says the policeman. 'No,' she says. 'Pair of socks.'

And the whale, the squid and the octopus. And the tramp and the cold rice pudding. I cannot bring myself to repeat some of the punch-lines, but they're all in Brian's book of jokes, *I say, I say, I say*. If most of us were to repeat them no one would laugh. In Brian's mouth they became uproarious.

A cricketing story about a hung-over wicket-keeper called 'Hopper' Levitt leads on naturally to the one about the proselytising teetotaller who compares what happens to worms in a glass of whisky and a glass of water – punch-line: 'If you've got worms, don't drink whisky.'

'Humility,' he says, suddenly and without warning, 'I think humility is very important and I learnt the hard way.' And he tells how he kept wicket in charity and 'fun' games to most of the great bowlers of his day and how at the Dragon School, Oxford, he stumped someone off Richie Benaud, thought he had performed adroitly – only to be congratulated, by the school bursar, on 'the sporting way you tried to give him time to get back'.

Audiences do love people telling jokes against themselves

and Brian does it with aplomb, even though by this stage of the evening he is beginning to lack true conviction.

For a while Brian risks some almost serious analytical cricket material on the subject of captaincy. He describes how Mike Brearley made Willis bowl uphill and into the wind at Headingley in 1981 and reveals that Brearley, a trained psychotherapist, said he did it in order to make Willis angry. This is not a joke, and suddenly one senses a confusion in the audience, as if they don't understand why at the end of the anecdote there appears to be nothing to laugh at. One or two actually let out a nervous titter. Brian swiftly makes amends by producing a well-known Keith Miller nugget: the time when Miller led his eleven on to the field of play and one of them pointed out that there were twelve men present.

'Well,' said Miller, not pausing in his stride, 'tell one of them to bugger off.'

After captaincy Brian considers umpires and makes a plea for fair play. Again he essays some serious stuff but seems to realise when he has gone too long without a laugh and, shamelessly, says, 'Did you hear about the Irishman? Caught a brilliant catch at second slip . . . missed it on the action replay.'

I'm losing track of the links now. Indeed most of the links seem to be no more complicated than 'another lovely story', which brings us naturally to the very hoary number about the Duke of Norfolk as manager of Ted Dexter's 1963 MCC tour of Australia. ('I hope it's true,' says Brian in a rare moment of uncertainty.) It involves horse-racing, illegal stimulants, sugar lumps and the final admonition from trainer to jockey that if anyone were to pass him in the final two furlongs 'It's either the Duke of Norfolk or myself.' Not many cricket dinners pass without that being told after the meal.

Cue for another Duke of Norfolk story. This one is about the Duke's butler, Meadows – most of Brian's manservants seem to be called Meadows – who is required to make a tricky umpiring decision and delivers the unusual verdict: 'His Grace is not in.' (High winds, if not exactly gales, of laughter.) The next story is cued in by 'apropos of that'. This is the one about the umpire McGuinness in Australia during Peter May's tour. Brian's friend, Tom Crawford, sometime captain of Kent second XI, was dining with no less than Don Bradman and vouchsafed criticism of Australian umpires in general and McGuinness in particular. He suggested the problem was that Australian umpires never played first-class cricket. The Don was outraged. 'McGuinness,' he protested, 'used to play for South Australia till his eyesight went.' This is a hard-core Johnston story, though like many such it varies in the details of the telling.

Cricket is the theme and since, for Brian as for others, cricket is a metaphor for life, almost anything goes. 'Just before we stop', Brian takes us back to the Friday of the Oval Test match in 1991. Bad light stopped play at 6.30 and Peter Baxter asked Brian to go through the scorecard with Jonathan Agnew. You sense that this is the moment for which his audience has been waiting all evening.

It doesn't look funny on paper. Listening to it, however, you cannot help being infected with the hysteria of the moment following this exchange regarding the unfortunate dismissal of Ian Botham:

Johnston: He tried to do the splits over it and unfortunately the inner part of his thigh must have just removed the bail.
Agnew: He just didn't quite get his leg over.

And the rest has become broadcasting history – one of the

most out of control examples of live 'corpsing' ever heard on radio. Not that funny on paper. Not that funny out loud either until Brian starts to giggle and becomes effectively helpless.

The tape recording is punctuated by mass audience laughter, almost as helpless as the commentator's, and when Brian switches off, just after the moment when he has resumed enough control to say that he has stopped laughing, he says that episode demonstrates that cricket is fun. 'The giggle went round the world,' he says. 'And I don't think it's a bad thing.'

And that's it. He thanks everyone for coming. He says he hopes everyone has enjoyed meeting him. He's enjoyed meeting them. And he finishes on a little song which he manages, unaccompanied and more or less in tune:

Columbus discovered America
Hudson discovered New York
Benjamin Franklin discovered the spark
Which Edison discovered would light up the dark
Oh Marconi discovered the wireless
Telegraph across the ocean blue
But the greatest discovery
Was when you discovered me
And I . . . discovered . . . you . . .

After which, sounding diffident and almost embarrassed, he murmurs 'Thank you very much', almost as if it is he who should have been paying money to perform rather than his audience to be enthralled.

Bald print cannot do justice to these lines as they sound when you hear the old man singing. For the first time in the evening he does suddenly seem eighty and tired, and yet the singing is obviously the right climax and he manages the croon with a defiant gusto, going out with a climactic 'you . . . ooh . . . ooh' which would have surely brought a smile to the lips of Bud Flanagan and certainly brings his audience to its feet. The final applause is loud and heartfelt and warm with affection. Hindsight, of course, gives the moment an extra poignancy, for we know now that this was a swansong and a final bow.

He was delivering his last hurrah.

Like so much of his life, the performance defies conventional critical analysis. As Roy Hudd has written – and other 'professionals' confirm – 'He had an infectious chortle that made you forgive him even the unforgivable, laughing at his own jokes. And, joy of joys, you knew if you could come up with something that really tickled him you'd be rewarded with his unforgettable collapse into helpless gibbering jelly.'

This is true. Brian broke all the rules, and a few more not yet invented. It's difficult to think of anyone else who could have got away with it, but he did more than that. The show was a triumph, and yet, if a thrusting young agent had gone to some smart impresario and said, 'I've got this eighty-year-old man, not a stage performer, and he has this act – it's two hours, solo – he tells a lot of very old jokes; reminisces about his life and times; lays down some adages about the game of cricket; plays a handful of old tape recordings; and, er, that's it,' the impresario would have laid down his cigar, fixed the agent with a beady smile and said, 'You must be joking.'

Which, of course, Brian was. But the joke certainly wasn't on him.

16

Close of Play

Four Score and One

The irony is that just as the one-man show fulfilled Brian and gave him as much pleasure as anything he ever did, so it was the show, in many people's opinion, that helped to kill him.

The performance would have been gruelling even for someone trained and experienced as a stand-up comedian or raconteur. It would have taxed a Peter Ustinov or a Victor Borge. Two hours with a live audience of hundreds, no notes, no props, just you, talking, with only a couple of tape recordings and a single interval to alleviate the pressure: that is tough going. Despite his lifetime of broadcasting he wasn't really used to this. Although he was an accomplished after dinner speaker, most of his career had been spent observing and reporting. Of course he had always been a natural spinner of yarns and teller of jokes, but usually as asides to interviews and commentaries. Now he had to carry the whole two hours on his own shoulders.

And Brian was eighty.

Brian knew that Pauline was anxious about the strain he was putting himself under. At one point he even admitted to

Clare that he wasn't telling her mother quite how many he was doing because he knew she would fret – as indeed she would have done. Don Mosey was a guest at Boundary Road that autumn and thought Brian was looking unusually tired. He warned him that he was in danger of overdoing it, but Brian shrugged it off with a 'Don't be ridiculous, Alderman.'

He didn't seem able to say no. In part it was the wretched school-fees. Each show earned a thousand pounds, and every thousand went into the grandchildren's piggy bank in order to pay for their education. Brian had enjoyed a private education and so had all five of his own children. He was determined that his grandchildren should have the same privilege. Since grandfather was in a position to earn more money than any other member of the family, then he should cash in. In any case, as he kept saying, he loved it. He was having the time of his life.

Pauline and I checked through his diary for that final year. It is fairly cryptic, not to say barely legible, but the basic message is clear enough.

He was overdoing it.

In March 1993 he made his debut to an unprecedented sell-out audience in Chichester and then went on to play Taunton, Leatherhead, Colchester, Hounslow and Richmond (Yorkshire). There were a further nine in April and four in May. As with the March schedule, the venues were scattered all over England. There was no sense of geographical planning. A more reasonable routine would, for instance, have bracketed Chichester with Portsmouth and Southampton, Taunton with Yeovil and Bath. Instead he seems to have been racketing about the country in the most arduous way imaginable.

He broke off in the summer because of cricket. This

included six five-day Test matches around the country. Each one involved a full day beginning at 9.30 in the morning and ending well after stumps were drawn. Less visible were the matches at Wormsley, the sumptuous new ground of his friend John Paul Getty. I remember seeing Brian on the opening day, when he was there in his capacity as match manager for the Getty team. He had persuaded Imran Khan to captain the home team, and together with Getty, ensured that the guest list was star-studded. Not only were Michael Caine and John Mortimer in attendance, with their wives. At one moment, sitting together on a bench in front of the thatched pavilion were the Queen Mother, the Prime Minister, Getty himself and Denis Compton. Rarefied stuff!

Throughout the season Brian made the fifty-minute Sunday drive to Wormsley, arriving by 10 a.m. and not leaving until at least 7.15. Quite apart from being team manager, he cast a supervisory eye over all the arrangements from the wicket to the scorebook. Being Brian he took it seriously. He wasn't exactly in charge but he clearly felt responsible. Quite apart from anything else it meant that the regular family Sunday lunches were ruled out. Pauline was unhappy about this, but Brian felt a commitment to Getty, so, during that period, Sundays were dedicated to Wormsley rather than family.

There were also performances of his *Trivia Test Match* radio programme with Tim Rice and Willie Rushton and work for his charities, including especially the blind.

In early autumn Brian and Pauline also crammed in a flying visit to Hong Kong for the six-a-side tournament in Kowloon. Brian took the opportunity to order a few more of his beloved silk shirts, as well as a blue suit for his stage show. Sadly he never got to wear them.

Small wonder that the indefatigible octogenarian was beginning to suffer. For almost the first time in his life he was feeling physically low. He had sciatica on the right side. It caused him pain and made him uncharacteristically depressed. He saw his doctors but they didn't seem able to alleviate the pain. He was suffering.

From 6 October to 21 November he performed thirteen one-man shows. On the 22nd Brian made a BBC recording at the Paris theatre. On the 23rd he was at the Lady Taverners' wine tasting; two days later he did the show in Newcastle and next day he spoke at a London dinner. Two days after that he was at the Water Rats Ball at Grosvenor House, followed on the 29th by the Sportsman of the Year Awards at BBC TV Centre and on the 30th an eightieth birthday luncheon for his old friend and colleague Reg Hayter. That same evening he read one of the lessons at a Carol Service for the United Response.

No respite was planned. Between 2 December and 17 December he was scheduled to be the guest speaker at seven different luncheons – one every two days. In the New Year, aged 81, he was already booked in for fourteen luncheons and eighteen of the evening one-man shows.

It was too much.

On the morning of 2 December the alarm went off at 7.45 and Brian went to his bathroom; performed his ablutions; brought Pauline a breakfast tray and a *Daily Mail* and complained of mild indigestion. To cope with this he took one of her Bisodol tablets.

He had a lunch-time speaking engagement in Bristol and the cab was calling at 9 to take him to Paddington Station. Shortly before, dressed scrupulously as ever in his light brown check suit, he told Pauline that he was still feeling slightly indigested. He took another of her tablets, kissed her good-bye and said he hoped he'd be back around 6 p.m.

Twenty minutes later Pauline received the worst telephone call of her life. The cabbie's passenger had collapsed. The taxi-driver had taken him to the nearest hospital, the Maida Vale, where there was no casualty department nor intensive care. The doctors there pummelled Brian back into life on the floor of the reception area and then within minutes an ambulance had whisked him away to St Mary's Paddington which had all the sophisticated facilities necessary.

Meanwhile in Boundary Road Pauline waited for the faithful Cally to arrive on schedule at 9.30, whereupon the two sped to Paddington.

Brian was in intensive care, flat out, wired up, comatose, light years from the breezy bloke who had left home an hour or so earlier complaining only of mild indigestion.

'That's not Brian,' thought Pauline when she saw him lying there. 'It can't be.'

The following days sound nightmarish. The doctors warned that because Brian had been unconscious for some time following the initial attack he might have suffered brain damage. Pauline phoned the BBC to tell them that he had collapsed and the news was given out on the air that morning at 11. The get well messages started to flood in almost immediately. The response was overwhelming.

Three days later he had recovered sufficiently to come off the ventilator and move to an intensive care ward with eight others. Pauline wasn't sure whether or not he recognised her. She hopes so. She visited him morning and afternoon, held his hand and talked to him, but never knew how much of what she said actually got through.

On the 10th he was well enough to be moved to a mixed

211

ward of twenty. But he wasn't himself. Pauline winced when people walked by his bed and called out in a cheery way, 'How's the cricket going, Brian?' He didn't know how the cricket was going, nor anything else.

A few days later he was well enough to be moved from St Mary's to King Edward VIII's Hospital. Pauline showed me a picture she particularly treasures of him looking as frail as he had done all those years before when he had been invalided out of Brazil. He is gazing at her from his wheelchair with a seraphic smile. He obviously recognised her then.

On the 23rd, two days before Christmas, he was well enough to come home.

Christmas was made even more difficult to bear when another phone call told her that Barry and his wife and child had been involved in a car crash on their way to Clare's house in Balham. Someone had run into the back of their car on a slip road off the motorway. Nobody was seriously hurt, but coming on top of Brian's disaster it was a further shock. Meanwhile Ian was out of touch in South America and only phoned just before Christmas. This was the first he knew of his father's heart attack.

They were bitter-sweet days. Pauline described that Christmas with just the two of them and 'a lovely New Zealand girl called Sarah', as the saddest day of her life. One day she took him down to Lord's and they walked round the ground arm-in-arm. Brian seemed quite unaware of his surroundings until, in front of the pavilion, she pointed up to the commentary box.

'What's that?' she asked.

'Test Match Special,' he said.

Throughout these days Brian was often confused. They managed a few gentle walks together but sometimes he would

212

try to have a bath and dress himself because he thought he had some engagement to fulfil. 'What are you doing, darling?' Pauline asked once when she found him sitting in the drawing-room in a curious muddle of pyjamas and suit and tie. 'You know what I'm doing,' he said, 'I have to present these prizes.' Indeed he had a remorseless schedule ahead of him. Sometimes he talked of meeting his brother Michael, dead these twenty years or more, and of his mother. He referred to them both as if they were still alive and well. Pauline sometimes felt this meant that he was about to join them in some other world and felt reassured by this in an odd superstitious way. Once he reached out and took her in his arms and said piteously, 'I feel as if I'm in a terrible deep hole and I don't know how to get out of it.'

He never did. Or rather he got out of the hole in the only way possible.

Early in the New Year, peacefully and mercifully, aged 81, he died.

Curtain Calls

They buried him on a Monday on the hillside at Swanage overlooking the sea. He first lived in the county in 1923 and for years the Isle of Purbeck had been the nearest he got to a real family retreat. 'If I were asked which was my favourite county,' he used to say, 'I would have to plump for Dorset.'

The day before the interment it was raining hard, and Pauline, sensing intuitively that something was wrong, went to the cemetery to see that the grave was properly prepared. To her dismay she found that it had been dug in quite the wrong place. The undertakers had misread the map, looked at it upside down, and prepared Brian's final resting-place far from where it was originally supposed to be.

Some distraught widows would have shrugged bitterly and accepted fate, but Pauline, being Pauline, dragged a couple of grave-diggers away from their weekend off and supervised them in the downpour as they re-dug the grave in the proper place. The funeral was small and private, and there he lies in a corner of his favourite county, in a prime site with a fine view.

I don't know where one would have expected him to be

buried. That outsize public personality might have seemed to cry out for Lord's itself or a corner of Westminster Abbey, but there was something very apt about a quiet hill-side with a sea view in rural Dorset. This had always been a private, secluded place for this most English of Englishmen. It was to Swanage that he had always retired to recharge his batteries, to relax with his family and take time off from the demands of the world. It was a fitting place for his final rest.

There is a Purbeck stone there now among the flowers planted by Pauline. On one side there are crossed cricket bats, and on the other a BBC microphone and stumps. The inscription reads:

Brian Johnston CBE MC
24 June 1912 – 5 January 1994

Adored husband, father and grandpa
Broadcaster and author
Sadly missed by all who loved him
for his kindness and humour

'It's been a lot of fun'

Gone to the great pavilion in the sky

Perhaps there is no such thing as a normal death accompanied by conventional grief and everyday tributes. Many widows receive letters of condolence, but few have the hundreds that were sent to mourn Brian. They came from close friends, from casual acquaintances and people Brian never met but who felt they were friends because of his broadcasts. Everybody from Buckingham Palace to the London taxi ranks seemed to want to share in Pauline's sorrow.

Over the months she answered every letter and found it, as the bereaved so often do, both a chore and a solace. She was even more amazed when on the first anniversary of his illness and of his death the letters came again, not in quite the same numbers, but in quantity nonetheless, from people remembering that she was suffering a painful anniversary and wanting to offer comfort.

There were public tributes on radio and television, where the programme faded out with the recording of him and 'Aggers' giggling over Botham's failing to get his leg over. Some critics felt it a trivial way to memorialise him, but most agreed that it was a poignant conclusion, a vivid reminder of the zest and vitality which had illumined so many summers so recently.

Brian himself was a *Telegraph* rather than a *Times* reader, if only because he had a lifelong preference for the *Telegraph*'s crossword. Nevertheless he would probably have accepted that *The Times*, despite its recent dilution and loss of authority, remains the nearest Britain's ruling class has to its own noticeboard. Here he had 'tributes' on the front page and three separate personal assessments, from the sports essayist Simon Barnes, the word-pundit Philip Howard, and his old friend, the Thunderer's former cricket correspondent, John Woodcock. Each one had the word 'Johnners' in the headline. Woodcock said that 'the game of cricket has lost its best-loved friend'; Howard declared that 'he had more influence on the native tongue than most professors of English', and Barnes thought that 'it was his unique talent to share the same secret joke with everyone who owned a radio. That was what made him a great broadcaster; that is why he is mourned by millions who never met him but considered him a friend.'

This was heady stuff, though the traditionalist in Brian

217

would have been even more impressed by the fact that in addition to this avalanche of column inches *The Times* also gave him the lead obituary that day. It ran to half a page, which is pretty much what the paper would have given a cabinet minister or a former England cricket captain. That nickname was invoked again in the text, though he would have preferred the conventional formality of the opening sentence with its less familiar and more respectful reference to 'Brian Johnston, CBE, MC, cricket commentator, author and raconteur'. The final *Times* verdict was that 'When Johnners was behind the microphone all was right with the world.'

Then in mid-May came the packed memorial service at Westminster Abbey, an occasion which most people found moving and appropriate though a few of Brian's older and more conservative friends felt it sometimes crossed the boundaries of good form. This coincided with another success which was almost as astonishing, namely the valedictory *Summers Will Never Be the Same* – its title taken from a tribute by John Major. This volume of tributes to Brian, edited by Christopher Martin-Jenkins and Pat Gibson, clearly struck a chord, for within a year of his death it went through numerous editions, selling well over a hundred thousand copies and in the process benefiting Brian's favourite charities as well as his much-loved grandchildren.

This was not the only enduring memorial to the man. During the next few months Pauline planted a tree presented by the St John's Wood Society in the presence of the Deputy Lord Mayor of Westminster. The tree, in the churchyard of the parish church, would be visible from Lord's when fully grown. A day later Pauline named a Britannia Airways Boeing 767, 'The Brian Johnston CBE, MC'; and she christened a Brian Johnston broadcasting centre at the

Kennington Oval. At Lord's, unquestionably his favourite ground, there is also to be a permanent memorial to Brian in the form of a bench behind the Warner Stand.

By happy chance his old Oxford college, New College, were rebuilding their sports pavilion and in memory of their former captain of cricket, not to mention the scorer of that famous, be-macintoshed try, they decided that the building should be named 'The Brian Johnston Pavilion'.

His family wanted a memorial in Swanage, too. It transpired that Durlston Country Park had reclaimed a field which had been re-seeded to become a wildflower meadow as part of a nature walk. This had no name and it was therefore proposed and accepted *nem. con.* that it be called henceforth 'The Brian Johnston Meadow'.

One of Brian's little 'grace-notes' on *Test Match Special* was to instigate a 'champagne moment', when a bottle of sparkling nectar was presented in tribute to a particularly memorable '*je ne sais quoi*' (How sensible not to attempt. . .). Not a great innings, or a fine bowling performance, but a sudden flash of something special which stuck in the mind when mere statistics had been forgotten. This has now become, *in memoriam*, 'The Brian Johnston champagne moment'.

Such gestures are given to few.

However there are two ways in which he will live on after death in an even more appropriate manner. Throughout the year after his father's death Ian, returned from his South American safari and, at first without a full-time job, busied himself establishing a Brian Johnston Memorial Trust. The idea was to raise £5 million to be dispensed on the causes most dear to Brian's heart. The most important of these was the development of young cricketers, especially those boys who would not otherwise have the opportunity to learn the game.

Apart from this the principal beneficiaries would be the blind cricketers, for whom he had always had a specially soft spot; village cricket, which in some ways had always been, for him, the game's purest and most English form; and the acting profession, to which he himself had always aspired. He was all too well aware that old actors did not always provide adequately for their retirement, and his family think he would have enjoyed knowing that money raised in his name might alleviate the suffering of distressed thespians and music hall artistes. After all, he could easily have become one himself. Neil Durden-Smith, the PR consultant and old family friend, is the chair, and the patron is his friend and fellow *Neighbours* fan, John Paul Getty.

But in the end it was the spoken word that made Brian Johnston famous and endeared him to millions. Of course, by the end of his life, those inimitable features were as recognisable to millions as the sound he made and the words that he uttered. But he didn't win the nation's affection because of his looks. Nor, despite his many and successful books, because of his skill with the pen. He was, above all, a master of the spoken word. Not so much of the formal speech as the easy, apparently effortless chatter and conversation of the born broadcaster. As Philip Howard wrote, perceptively, Brian 'had cracked the simple secret in the broadcasting age, of chatting into a microphone as though it were sitting at ease on a deckchair beside him, rather than addressing it coldly and nervously as a mass media meeting'.

Brian loved the microphone and the microphone loved him. And thanks be to modern technology we have the best of him for ever. 'An Evening with Johnners' won a gold disc and was in the best-seller charts for weeks. The cassette of his BBC broadcasts, 'Johnners at the Beeb', released in May 1995, was an immediate number one best-seller and seems bound to emulate it. And my guess is that there is plenty yet to come.

So the sound of Brian lives on. It will be possible, for years to come, to curl up in an armchair and listen to that avuncular chortling voice, telling old jokes, describing ridiculous escapades and pranks or even, sometimes, serious state occasions. So in a sense summers *will* be the same again, because we have only to turn on the Walkman and the CD player to find him in the room again, just as he always was, laughing and smiling, and always keeping the dark side of life at bay, just as he always did, in public and private, when he was alive.

For me, as I suspect for many others, he will remain the ever genial uncle, always spreading happiness and optimism, as he did most spectacularly and courageously during the war when he came to the rescue of his comrades in their crippled tanks, cracking jokes and laughing, as always. Like many favourite uncles, too, he will always preserve a decent privacy. Part of the fascination of Brian Johnston was that he allowed many of us to get close to him, but few if any to become too close for his own comfort.

As the psychotherapist said when I laid out the salient facts of Brian's story in front of her, 'It's a strong life.'

Meanwhile the memory lingers on. In January 1995, England won a famous victory in Adelaide, with de Freitas, in particular, producing the sort of swashbuckling performance which Brian would have admired. Just after the match I got a postcard with views of the Adelaide Oval postmarked 'Australia Day'. It was from Pauline. She wrote: 'Lots of Aussies come up to me here and say how much they miss Brian's voice.'

Brian would have enjoyed that.

Index